Y0-BSF-225

DELICATE LACE

Rose Table Center

Instructions on page 40 (76cm in diameter).

Filet Lace Cushion Covers
Instructions on page 33 (41cm square).

Pineapple-pattern Tablecloth
Instructions on page 42 (130cm in diameter).

Square Tablecloth
Instructions on page 35 (115cm square).

Doily, Coasters and Tray Mat

Instructions for Doily on page 47 (32cm in diameter).
Instructions for Coasters on page 49 (about 11cm in diameter).
Instructions for Tray Mat on page 47 (36cm in diameter).

DECORATE YOUR HOME WITH LACE

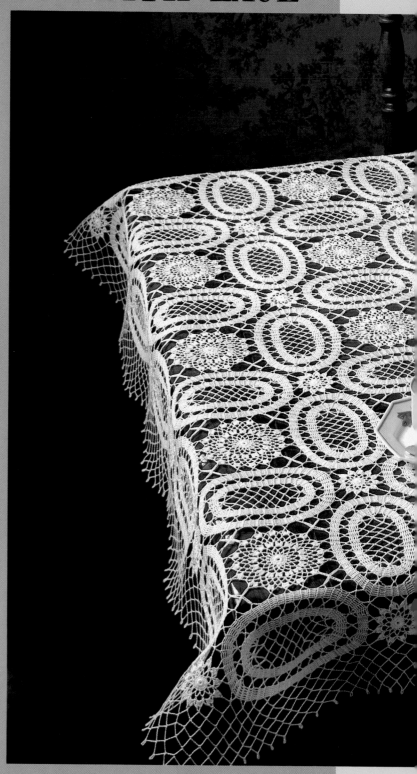

Oval-motif Tablecloth

Instructions on page 51 (153cm by 115cm).

Flower-motif Table Center
Instructions on page 38 (77cm by 41cm).

Lily Table Runner
Instructions on page 50 (151cm by 34.5cm).

Clematis Table Runner
Instructions on page 54 (96cm by 26cm).

Tablecloth

Instructions on page 64 (131.5cm by 100cm).

Piano Cover

Instructions on page 56 (150cm by 38cm).

Pineapple-pattern Cushion Covers and Matching Table Center

Instructions on page 58 (Cushion Cover, 46cm in diameter;
Table center, 49cm in diameter).

Butterfly Table Center

Instructions on page 60 (66cm in diameter).

Diamond-pattern Chair Back, Sofa Back and Matching Cushion Covers

Instructions on page 61 (Sofa Back, 115cm by 70cm; Chair Back, 43.5cm by 70cm; Cushion Cover, 45cm in diameter).

FOR THE BEDROOM

Doily
Instructions on page 66 (34cm in diameter).

Doily

(Top)Instructions on page 65 (28cm in diameter).
(Bottom)Instructions on page 67 (32cm in diameter).

Bedspread

Instructions on page 78 (208cm by 166.5cm).

Tablecloth

Instructions on page 69 (113cm square).

LACE AND COTTON COMBINATIONS

Tray Mat
Instructions on page 68 (31cm by 27cm).

Pillows

Instructions on page 88
(A,B & E.40cm square; C.42cm square; D.48cm by 37cm).

27

Collars (A, B)
Instructions on page 71 (Width. 7.5cm).

Lace Edging (C-G)
Instructions on page 73 (Width: C.4cm; D.6.5cm; E.3cm; F.2.5cm; G.5cm).

Doily
Instructions on page 75 (45cm by 22.5cm).

Tissue Case
Instructions on page 76 (13cm by 10.5cm).

Cosmetic Case
Instructions on page 76(16cm by 11cm).

Compact Case
Instructions on page 77(10cm in diameter).

Bedspread
Instructions on page 83 (274cm by 182cm).

Curtain

Instructions on page 86 (120cm by 34cm).

INSTRUCTIONS

Filet Lace Cushion Covers, shown on pages 2 & 3.

MATERIALS AND EQUIPMENT: (FOR ONE COVER):
Mercerized crochet cotton, No. 40, 110g white. Steel crochet hooks, sizes 0.90mm and 1.50mm. Pink (blue, yellow) cotton satin, 90cm by 45cm. 45cm-square inner cushion stuffed with kapok.

FINISHED SIZE: 41 cm square. Width of ruffle, 4.5cm.
GAUGE: 10cm = 14 sps; 10cm = 14 rows. Size of Flower:

See diagram.

DIRECTIONS: Use size 0.90mm hook for making Leaves, Flower, Front & Back. Use size 1.50mm hook for making cord. For Flower: Ch 6, sl st in first ch to form ring. Rnd 1: Ch 1, sc 8 in ring, end with sl st. Rnd 2: Ch 4, 4-tr popcorn, (ch 3, 5-tr popcorn) 7 times, ch 3, end with sl st. Rnd 3: Ch 1, (sc 1, ch 4) 8 times, end with sl st. Rnd 4: Ch 1, (sc 1, hdc 1, dc 3, hdc 1, sc 1) 8 times, end with sl st. Rnd 5: Ch 6, (sc in back of work between sc of next 2 petals, ch 5) 7 times, end with sl st. Rnds 6-11: Following chart, work in same manner as Rnds 4-5, increasing ch and adding tr for petals. Rnd 12: Ch 1, (sc 1, ch 8) 7 times, end with sl st. Continue to work for Front: Rnd 1: Ch 7, (tr 1, ch 3) 3 times, tr 1, ch 7, (tr 1, ch 3) 5 times, tr 1, ch 7, (tr 1, ch 3) 5 times, tr l, ch 7, (tr 1, ch 3) 5 times, tr 1, ch 7, tr 1, ch 3, end with sl st. Rnd 2: Ch 6, tr 1, *(ch 3, tr l), repeat from * all around increasing ch 1 at corners. Rnds 2-26; Work in filet crochet following chart. Work 1 rnd of sc for edging. For Leaf: Ch 20. Rnd 1: Ch 1, sc 37. Rnd 2: Ch 1, rib st 17 (work same as sc but insert hook in back of st only), ch 1, rib st 17. Rnds 3-7: Work following chart.

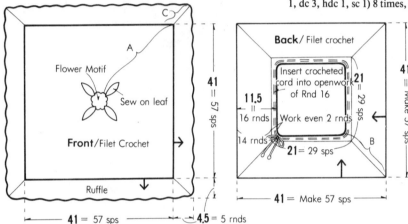

To work Flower Motif and Filet Crochet

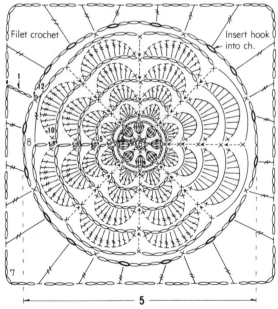

※ Sc in back of work between petals on Rnds 5,7,9 and 11

Leaf Make 4

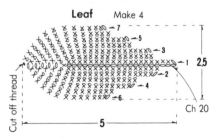

Crocheted Cord 100cm long
Use 2 strands of thread and 1.50mm hook

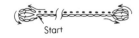

Start

After working for Front, continue to work for Back. Work following chart until 16th Rnd is completed. Dec from Rnd 1 to Rnd 14 and work even Rnds 15 & 16. Follow chart and work 5 rnds for ruffle with right side facing. Make 4 leaves and 4 antennae. Sew them in place. Following chart, make cord with 2 strands of thread using 1.5mm hook. Insert crocheted cord into openwork of Rnd 16. Make cushion cover with cotton satin, 43cm square. Insert inner cushion stuffed with kapok into cotton satin cover. Cover with lace.

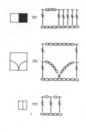

Front

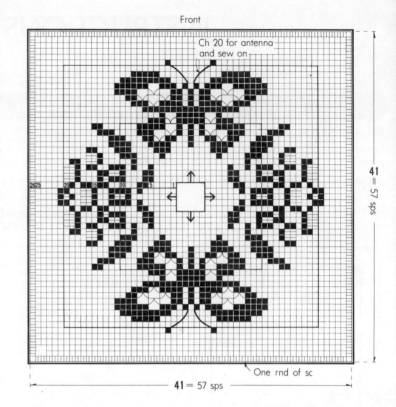

Ch 20 for antenna and sew on

41 = 57 sps

41 = 57 sps

One rnd of sc

A. Chart for Increasing at Corners of Front

C. Chart for Ruffle and Increasing

B. Chart for Decreasing at Corners of Back

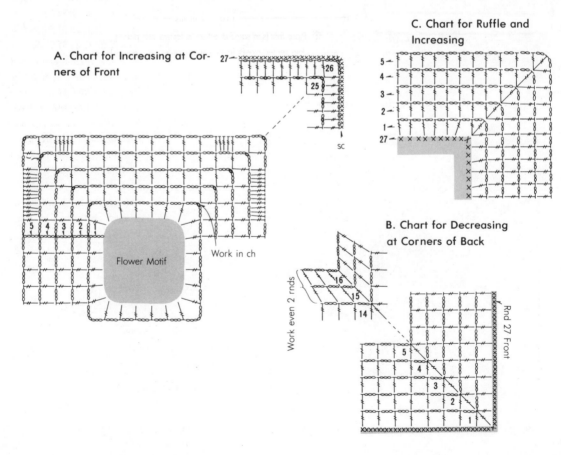

Flower Motif

Work in ch

sc

Work even 2 rnds

Rnd 27 Front

Square Tablecloth, shown on page 6.

MATERIALS AND EQUIPMENT: Mercerized crochet cotton, No. 40, 370g white. Steel crochet hook size 0.90mm.

FINISHED SIZE: 115cm square.

GAUGE: 10cm = 21 sps; 10cm = 21 rows.

SIZE OF MOTIF: 14cm square.

DIRECTIONS: For Motifs A & B: Ch 91 to make 30 sps plus 1st. Work 30 rows following chart. Make 17 pieces of Motif A and 16 pieces of Motif B. Following diagram, join Motifs A & B as shown with arrows from 1 to 4. Attach new thread at corner of Motif A, center top, and work one rnd of filet crochet. Work in lacet st for 6 rnds around center motifs. Then attach new thread and complete each triangle in lacet st. Join motifs for border following chart on page 38. Work one rnd in dc around square to join border motifs. Work 4 rnds of edging.

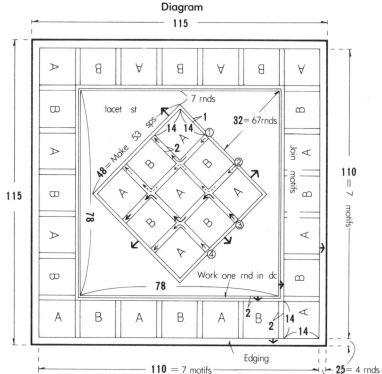

Diagram

※ Place motifs in same direction as letters are placed
Join center motifs in numerical order as shown by arrows.

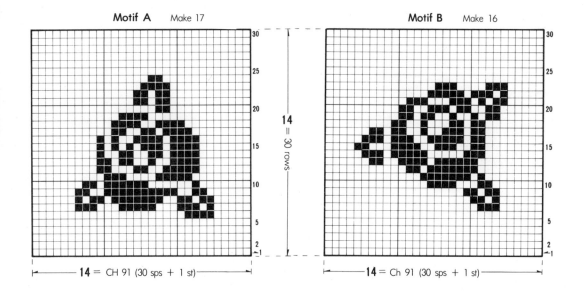

Motif A   Make 17

Motif B   Make 16

14 = 30 rows

14 = CH 91 (30 sps + 1 st)

14 = Ch 91 (30 sps + 1 st)

35

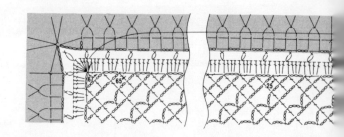

Lacet St

A	B		A	B
	Join border motifs with square, picking up 16 sts from each motif.			Center ↓

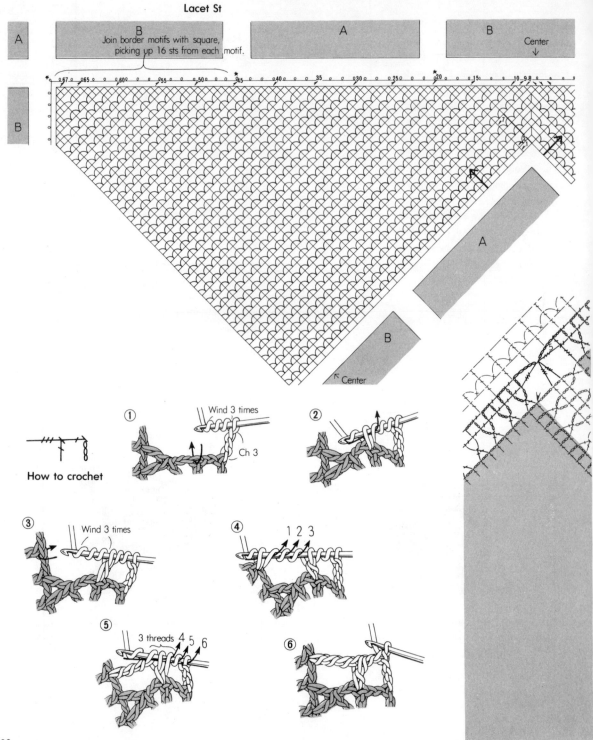

How to crochet

① Wind 3 times Ch 3

②

③ Wind 3 times

④ 1 2 3

⑤ 3 threads 4 5 6

⑥

Center

Chart for Joining Motifs and for Lacet St

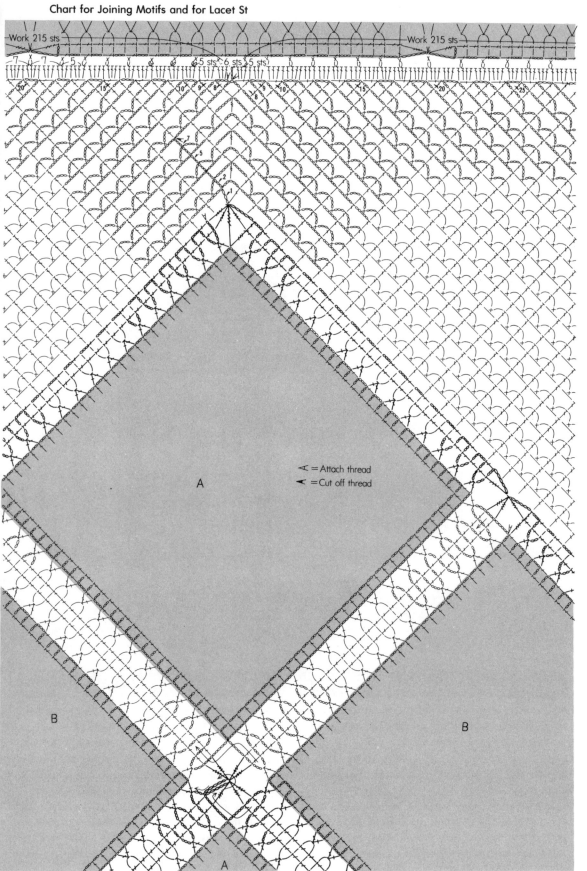

Work 215 sts   Work 215 sts

⊰ = Attach thread
◀ = Cut off thread

Chart for Joining Border Motifs and Edging

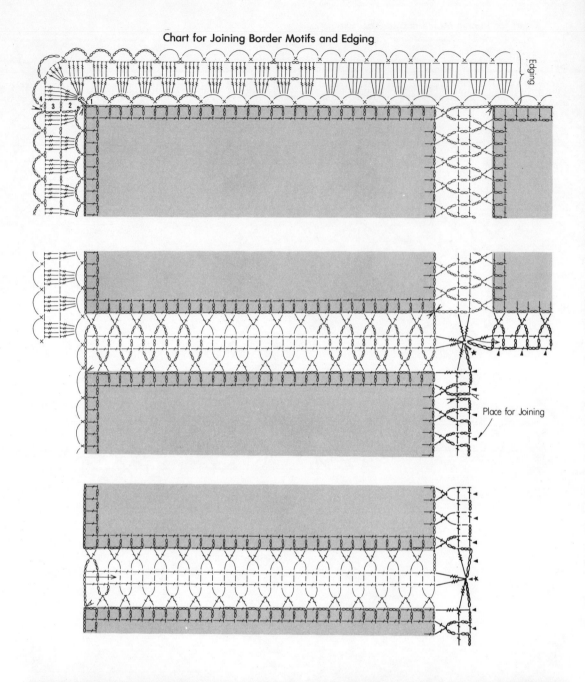

Edging

Place for Joining

Flower-motif Table Center, shown on page 12.

MATERIALS AND EQUIPMENT: Mercerized crochet cotton, No. 40, 90g white. Steel crochet hook size 0.90mm.

FINISHED SIZE: 77cm by 41cm.

GAUGE: 1 tr = 0.7cm.

SIZE OF MOTIFS: Motif A, 5cm square. Motif B, 3.5cm in diameter.

DIRECTIONS: For Motif A: Ch 12, join with sl st to form ring. Rnd 1: Ch 1, sc 24 in ring, end with sl st. Rnd 2: Ch 1, (sc 1, ch 7) 7 times, ch 3, tr 1, end with sl st. Rnd 3: (Ch 11, sc 1) 8 times, but omit last sc, end with sl st. Rnd 4: Sl st 3, ch

1, sc 5 in each ch, (3-tr puff, ch 7) 6 times, 3-tr puff 4 times. Cut off thread. Make 32 Motif As. Join 8 by 4 Motif As, working 3rd rnd of Motif Bs. For Motif B: Ch 12, join with sl st to form ring. Rnd 1: Ch 1, sc 24 in ring, end with sl st. Rnd 2: Ch 3, (ch 5, dc 1) 7 times, dc 1, ch 2, dc 1. Rnd 3: Ch 4, tr 2, (3-ch picot, tr 3, ch 1, sc in ch of Motif A to join, ch 1, tr 3) 7 times, 3-ch picot, tr 3, ch 1, sc 1, ch 1, end with sl st. Cut off thread. Join Motif B with Motif A as shown in chart, while working Rnd 3. Make and join 21 Motif Bs. Work 6 rnds of edging all around following chart.

Diagram

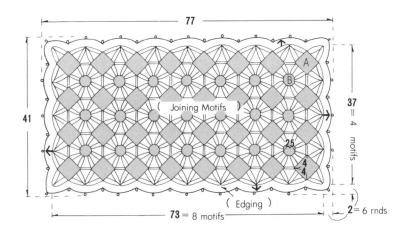

77

41

37 = 4 motifs

A

B

(Joining Motifs)

25

4
4

(Edging)

73 = 8 motifs

2 = 6 rnds

Join Motif As with Bs.

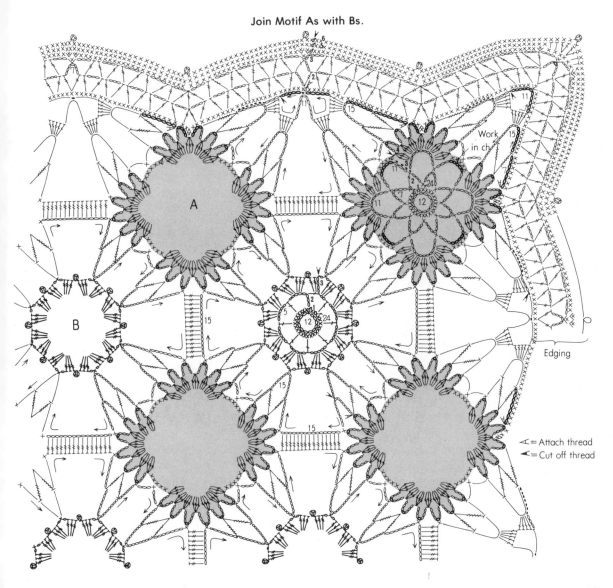

A

B

Work in ch

Edging

◁ = Attach thread
◀ = Cut off thread

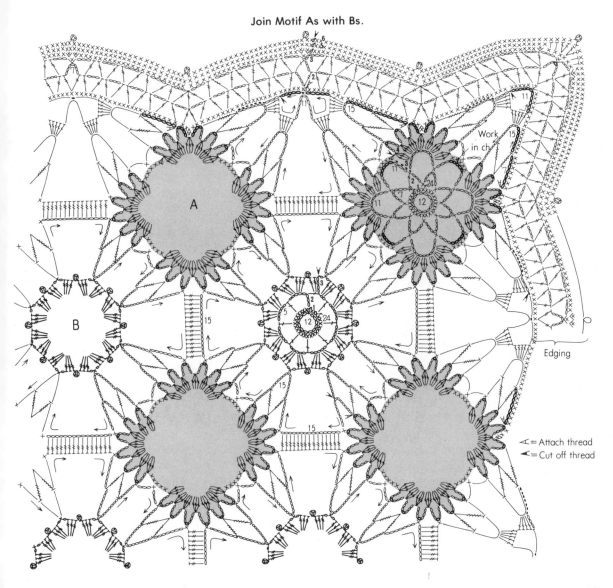

39

Rose Table Center, shown on page 1.

Attach thread

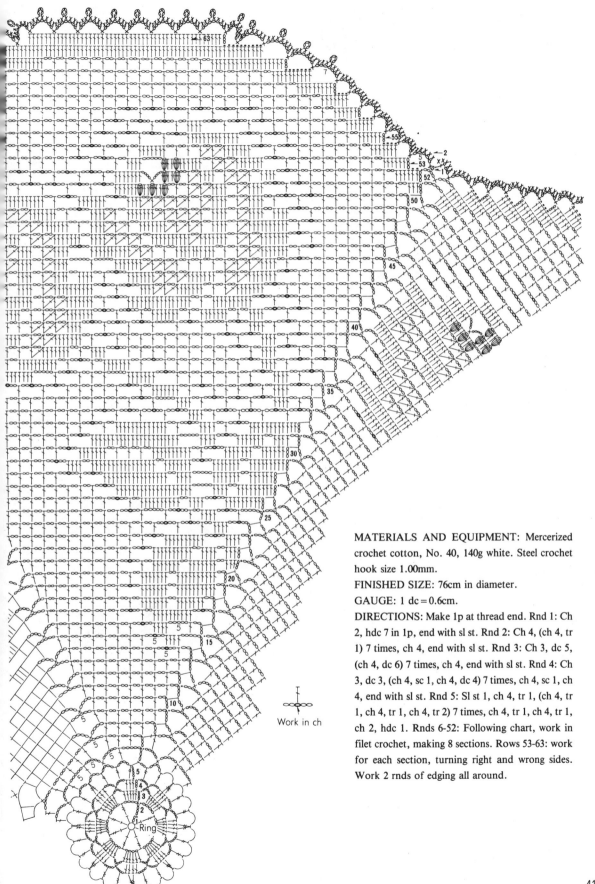

MATERIALS AND EQUIPMENT: Mercerized crochet cotton, No. 40, 140g white. Steel crochet hook size 1.00mm.

FINISHED SIZE: 76cm in diameter.

GAUGE: 1 dc = 0.6cm.

DIRECTIONS: Make 1p at thread end. Rnd 1: Ch 2, hdc 7 in 1p, end with sl st. Rnd 2: Ch 4, (ch 4, tr 1) 7 times, ch 4, end with sl st. Rnd 3: Ch 3, dc 5, (ch 4, dc 6) 7 times, ch 4, end with sl st. Rnd 4: Ch 3, dc 3, (ch 4, sc 1, ch 4, dc 4) 7 times, ch 4, sc 1, ch 4, end with sl st. Rnd 5: Sl st 1, ch 4, tr 1, (ch 4, tr 1, ch 4, tr 1, ch 4, tr 2) 7 times, ch 4, tr 1, ch 4, tr 1, ch 2, hdc 1. Rnds 6-52: Following chart, work in filet crochet, making 8 sections. Rows 53-63: work for each section, turning right and wrong sides. Work 2 rnds of edging all around.

41

Pineapple-pattern Tablecloth, shown on pages 4 & 5.

MATERIALS AND EQUIPMENT: Mercerized crochet cotton, No. 40, 250g white. Steel crochet hook size 0.90mm.

FINISHED SIZE: 130cm in diamter.

GAUGE: 1 dc = 0.5cm. 1 tr = 0.7cm.

DIRECTIONS: Ch 20, join with sl st to form ring. Rnd 1: Ch 1, sc 36 in ring, end with sl st. Rnd 2: Ch 3, dc 35, end with sl st. Rnd 3: Ch 3, dc 1, (ch 2, dc 3) 11 times, ch 2, dc 1, end with sl st. Rnds 4-48: Work following chart and make 12 pineapple patterns. Cut off thread. Rnds 49-91: Attach new thread and work following chart. After making small pineapples, work for 24 patterns. Cut off thread. Rnds 92-105: Attach thread and work following chart. Make 5-ch picots on Rnd 105.

= Attach thread
= Cut off thread

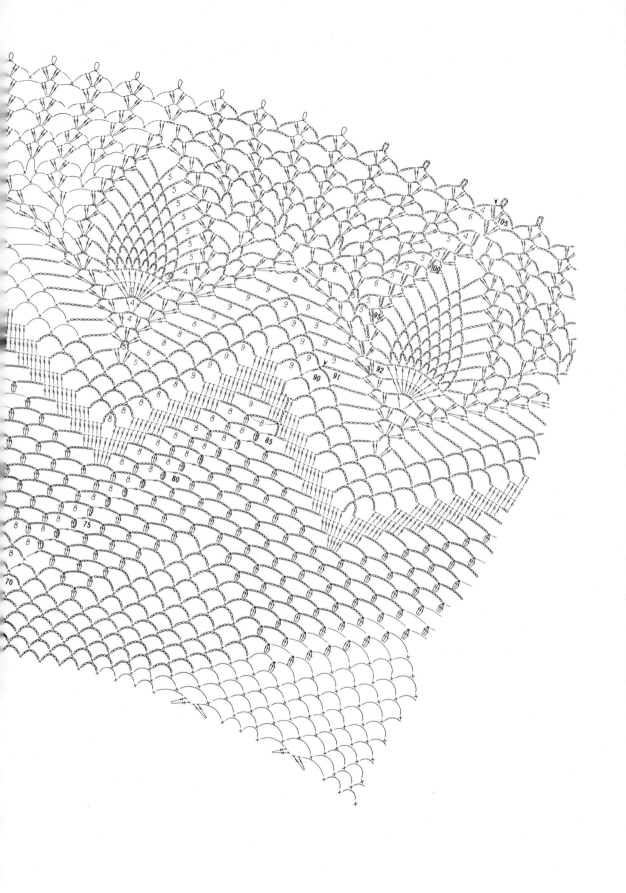

MATERIALS AND EQUIPMENT: Mercerized crochet cotton, No. 40, 60g white. Steel crochet hook sizes 1.00mm and 0.90mm.

GAUGE: 1 dc = 0.7cm. (with 1.00mm hook)

FINISHED SIZE: 48cm in diameter.

DIRECTIONS: With size 1.00mm hook, (ch 5, dc 1) 6 times, join with sl st to form ring. Rnd 1: Ch 3, (3-ch picot, ch 1, dc 2, ch 3, dc 2, ch 1, dc 1) 6 times, but omit last dc 1, end with sl st. Rnds 2-28: Work following chart. Rnds 29-31:Change to size0.90mm hook and work following chart.

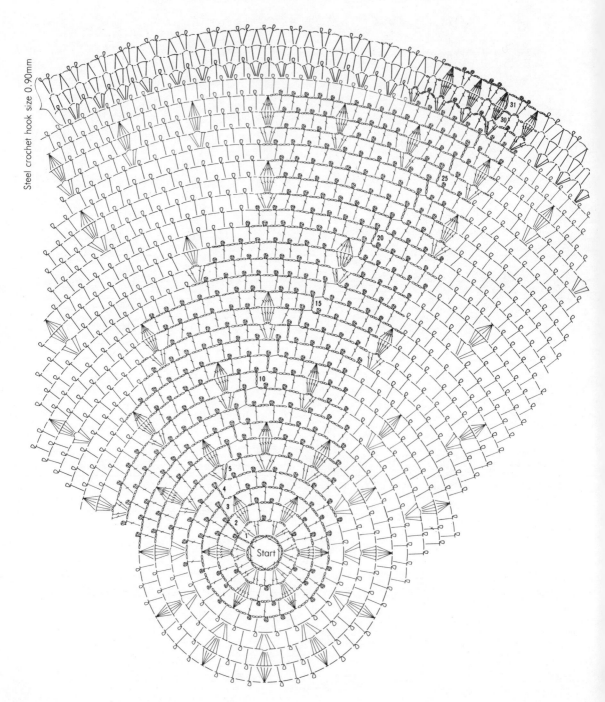

Steel crochet hook size 0.90mm

Doily, shown on page 8.

MATERIALS AND EQUIPMENT: Mercerized crochet cotton, No. 40, 15g white. Steel crochet hook size 0.90mm.
FINISHED SIZE: 32cm in diameter.
GAUGE: 1 tr = 0.7cm.

DIRECTIONS: Ch 16, join with sl st to form ring. Rnd 1: Ch 1, sc 32 in ring, end with sl st. Rnd 2: Ch 4, (ch 13, tr 1, ch 3, tr 1) 7 times, ch 13, tr 1, ch 1, hdc 1. Rnd 3: Ch 4, (ch 2, sc 3, ch 2, tr 1, ch 3, tr 1) 7 times, ch 2, sc 3, ch 2, tr 1, ch 1, hdc 1. Rnds 4-18: Work following chart.

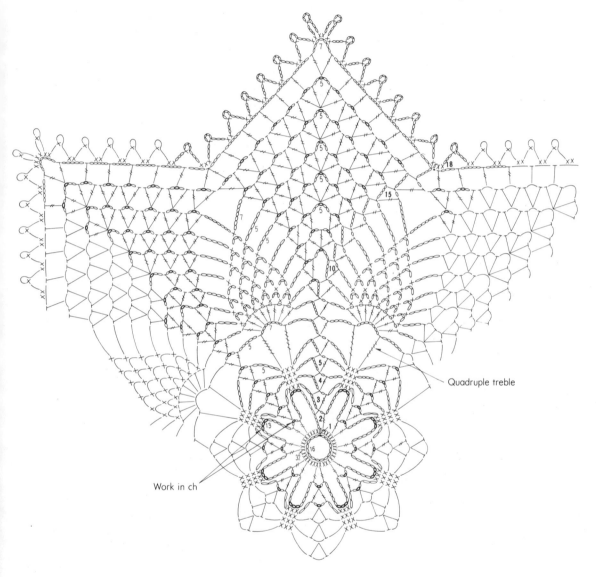

Quadruple treble

Work in ch

Tray Mat, shown on page 9.

MATERIALS AND EQUIPMENT: Mercerized crochet cotton, No. 40, 30g white. Steel crochet hook size 0.90mm.
FINISHED SIZE: 36cm in diameter.
GAUGE: 1 dc = 0.6cm.

DIRECTIONS: Make 1p at thread end. Rnd 1: ch 1, (sc 1, ch 16) 7 times, sc 1, ch 8, quintuple tr 1. Rnd 2: Ch 1, (sc 1, ch 6) 15 times, sc 1, ch 2, tr 1. Rnd 3: ch 3, dc 4, (ch 3, dc 1, ch 3, dc 1, ch 3, dc 5) 7 times, ch 3, dc 1, ch 3, dc 1, ch 3, end with sl st. Rnds 4-29: Work following chart.

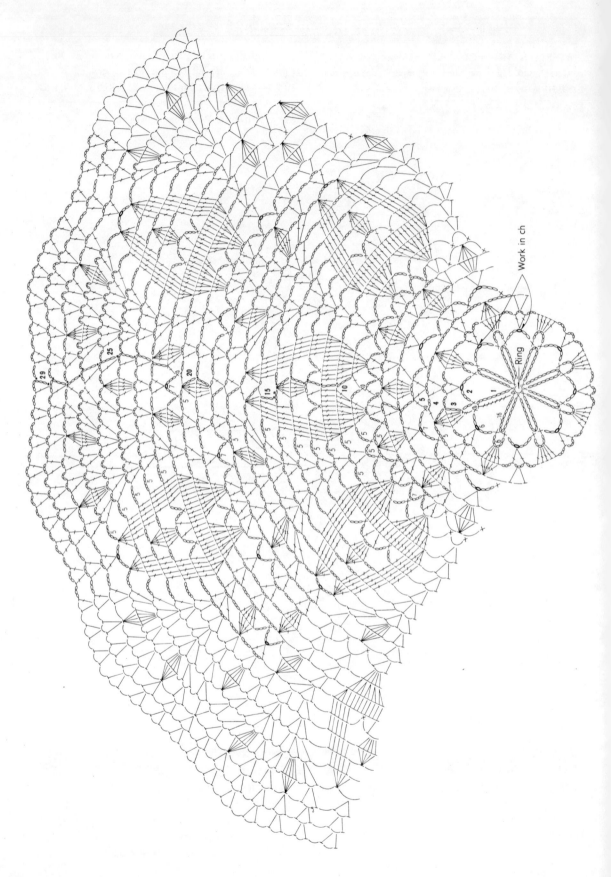

Work in ch

Ring

29   25   20   7   §15   10   5   4   3   2   1   16

48

MATERIALS AND EQUIPMENT (FOR ONE):
Mercerized crochet cotton, No. 40, 4g white. Steel crochet hook size 0.90mm.

FINISHED SIZE: 10.5cm in diameter.

GAUGE: 1 dc = 0.5cm.

DIRECTIONS: Make 1p at thread end. Rnd 1: Ch 3, (ch 2, dc 1) 7 times in 1p, ch 2, end with sl st. Rnd 2: ch 3, ch 2, dc 1, (ch 2, dc 1, ch 2, dc 1) 7 times, ch 2, end with sl st. Rnds 3-6: Work following chart. Rnd 7: (6-dc cluster, 6-ch picot, ch 3, dc 3, ch 3, sc 1, ch 3, dc 3, ch 3, sl st 1, ch 5, dc 1) 12 times, tr 1. Count first ch 3 as 1 dc. Rnd 8: Ch 3, (ch 6, sc 1, ch 7, sc 1, ch 6, dc 1) 12 times, but omit last dc, end with sl st. Cut off thread.

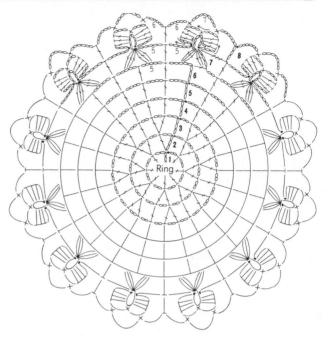

⟨Ruffled Coaster⟩

MATERIALS AND EQUIPMENT (FOR ONE) : Mercerized crochet cotton, No. 40, 6g white. Steel crochet hook size 0.90mm.

FINISHED SIZE: 11.5cm in diameter.

GAUGE: 1 dc = 0.5cm.

DIRECTIONS: Ch 8, join with sl st to form ring. Rnd 1: Ch 3, (ch 2, dc 1) 15 times in ring, ch 2, end with sl st. Rnds 2-6: Work following chart. Rnd 7: Ch 3, (ch 5, dc 1) 31 times, ch 5, end with sl st. Rnd 8: Ch 3, (ch 6, dc 1) 31 times, ch 6, end

with sl st. Rnd 9:*(tr 1, 3-ch picot, ch 1) 5 times in 6-ch 1p and 3 times over dc on Rnd 8, 4 times in 5-ch 1p of Rnd 7 (see details for Rnd 9). Count first ch 4 as 1 tr. Repeat from * all around. Cut off thread. Rnd 10: Attach new thread. Turn ruffle toward you and work *(sc 1, ch 1) 6 times, (sc 1, ch 2) 3 times, repeat from * all around, working in ch of Rnd 8. Lightly apply starch and press, bending 4 tr in 5-ch 1p toward center all around.

Chart for Rnd 9 Cut off thread

Bend 4tr in 5-ch 1p toward center.

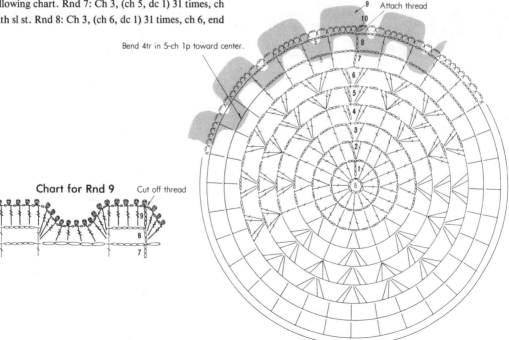

Lily Table Runner, shown on page 13, top.

MATERIALS AND EQUIPMENT: Mercerized crochet cotton, No. 40, 170g white. Steel crochet hook size 1.00mm.
FINISHED SIZE: 151cm by 34.5cm.
GAUGE: 10cm = 19.5 sps; 10cm = 20 rows.

DIRECTIONS: Ch 187 to make 62 sps plus 1st. Rows 1-148: Work following chart. Rows 149-296: Reverse chart and work back from Row 149 to Row 1. Work 2 rnds of edging.

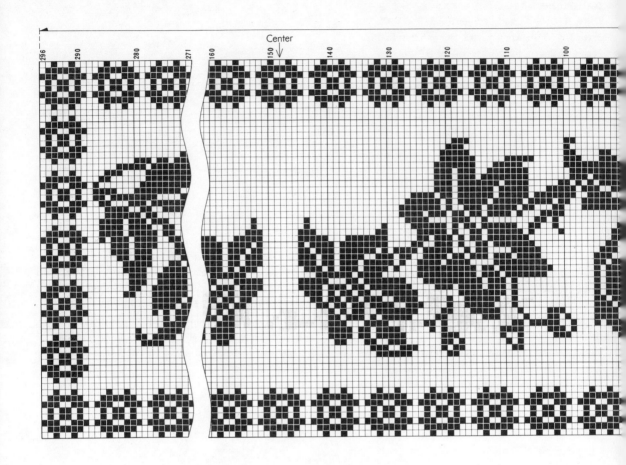

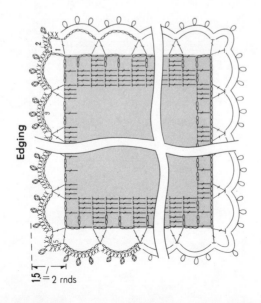

Edging

1.5 = 2 rnds

50

Oval-motif Tablecloth, shown on pages 10 & 11.

MATERIALS AND EQUIPMENT: Mercerized crochet cotton, No. 40, 430g white. Steel crochet hook size 1.00mm.

FINISHED SIZE: 153cm by 115cm.

SIZE OF MOTIFS: A, 15cm by 10cm oval; B, 9cm in diameter; C, 4cm in diameter.

GAUGE: 1 dc = 0.7cm.

DIRECTIONS: Make outer braid of Motif A first. Ch 6, (ch 7, dc 6) 52 rows, join with dc removing foundation ch. Then make inner braid. Ch 5, work 44 rows of (ch 3, join outer braid with sl st, ch 3, dc 5) for odd rows and (ch 7, dc 5) for even rows, join with dc removing foundation ch. Work 2 rnds to fill inside of inner braid, joining with sc. Make and join 82 motif As, following chart. For Motif B, ch 8, join

with sl st to form ring. Rnd 1: Ch 3, dc 31, end with sl st. Rnd 2: Ch 1, (sc 1, ch 5) 15 times, sc 1, ch 2, dc 1. Rnds 3-7: Work following chart. Rnd 8: Work following chart and join with Motif As. Make and join 35 Motif Bs with As. For Motif C, ch 6, join with sl st to form ring. Rnd 1: Ch 3, dc 23 in ring, end with sl st. Rnd 2: Ch 1, (sc 1, ch 5) 11 times, ch 2, hdc 1. Rnd 3: (sc 1, ch 5) 12 times, end with sl st. Rnd 4: Repeat (ch 3, dc 2, ch 3, dc 2, ch 3, sc 1) all around joining with Motif As. Change second ch between clusters to sl st or tr tr when joining. Make and join 48 Motif Cs with As as shown in chart. Work 6 rnds of edging.

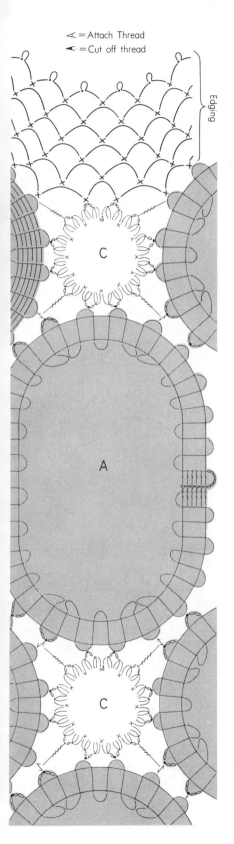

◁ = Attach Thread

◀ = Cut off thread

Edging

C

A

C

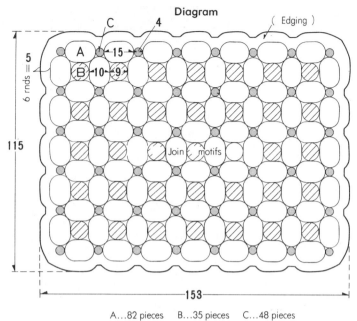

Diagram

C   4   (Edging)

A   →15→

6 rnds = 5   B →10→ →9→

115   Join motifs

153

A...82 pieces   B...35 pieces   C...48 pieces

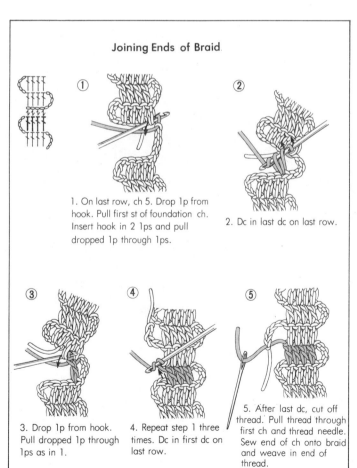

Joining Ends of Braid

①

②

1. On last row, ch 5. Drop 1p from hook. Pull first st of foundation ch. Insert hook in 2 1ps and pull dropped 1p through 1ps.

2. Dc in last dc on last row.

③

④

⑤

3. Drop 1p from hook. Pull dropped 1p through 1ps as in 1.

4. Repeat step 1 three times. Dc in first dc on last row.

5. After last dc, cut off thread. Pull thread through first ch and thread needle. Sew end of ch onto braid and weave in end of thread.

MATERIALS AND EQUIPMENT: Mercerized crochet cotton, No. 40, 60g white. Steel crochet hook size 1.00mm.

FINISHED SIZE: 96cm by 26cm.
GAUGE: 1 tr = 0.8cm.
SIZE OF MOTIF: See diagram.

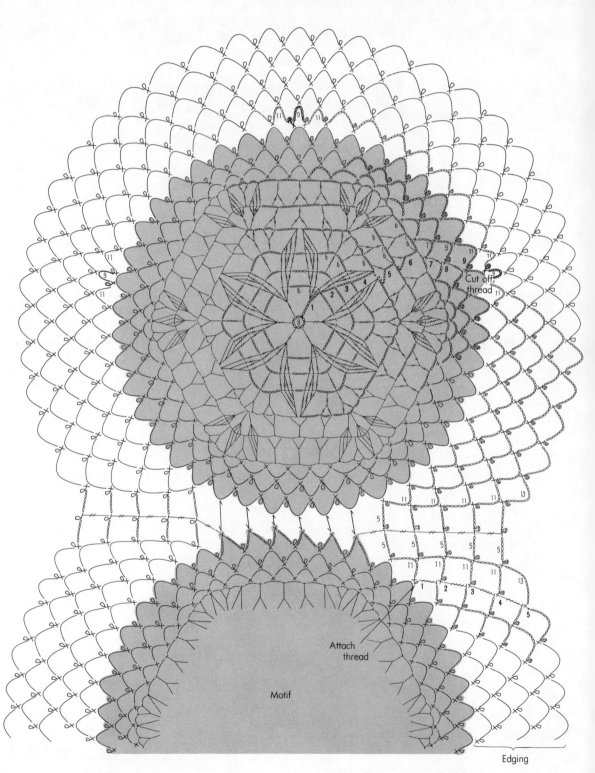

Cut off thread

Attach thread

Motif

Edging

54

DIRECTIONS: First Motif: Ch 8, join with sl st to form ring. Rnd 1: Ch 8, 3-tr cluster in 4th ch, (ch 6, tr tr 1, 3-tr in middle of tr tr [see next page for details,]) 5 times, ch 6,end with sl st. Rnds 2-6: Work following chart and form hex-agon. Rnds 7-9: Work following chart and form circle. Second Motif: Make in same manner as First Motif until Rnd 8. Join with First Motif working Rnd 9. Make and join 5 motifs in all. Work 5 rnds of edging.

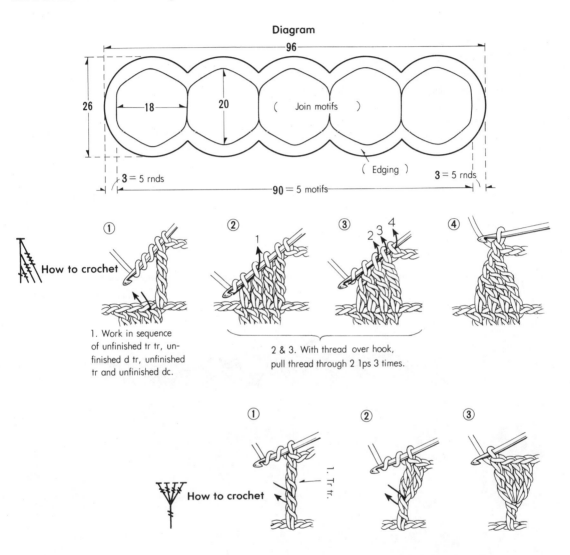

Diagram

96

26

18

20

(Join motifs)

3 = 5 rnds

(Edging)

3 = 5 rnds

90 = 5 motifs

How to crochet

① ② ③ ④

1. Work in sequence of unfinished tr tr, un-finished d tr, unfinished tr and unfinished dc.

2 & 3. With thread over hook, pull thread through 2 lps 3 times.

How to crochet

① ② ③

1. Tr tr.

MATERIALS AND EQUIPMENT: Mercerized crochet cotton, No. 40, 190g white. Steel crochet hook size 0.90 mm. White linen, 50cm by 158cm.

FINISHED SIZE: 150cm by 38 cm (crocheted area).

GAUGE: 10cm = 14 sps; 10cm = 21.5 rows.

DIRECTIONS: Ch 845 to make 211 sps plus 1 st. Work 82 rows following chart. To make one block: Dc in each of 4 sts. To make one space: Dc in st, ch 2, sk 2 sts, dc in next st. Work 1 row of edging in sc for three sides. Make hem as shown on page 57. Place crocheted lace on selvage of linen with one row overlapping and machine-stitch.

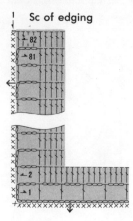

Sc of edging

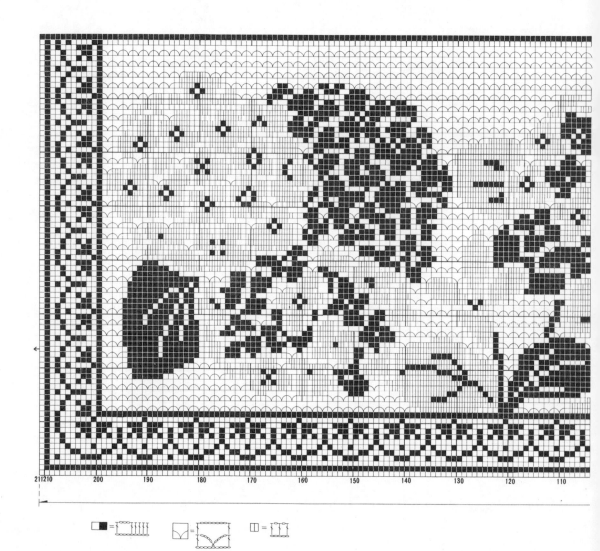

Diagram

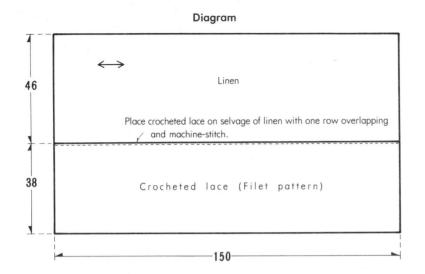

Linen

←→

46

Place crocheted lace on selvage of linen with one row overlapping and machine-stitch.

38

Crocheted lace (Filet pattern)

←————— 150 —————→

Hem

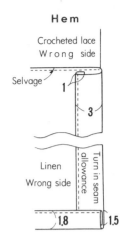

Crocheted lace
Wrong side

Selvage   1

3

Linen
Wrong side

Turn in seam allowance

1.8   1.5

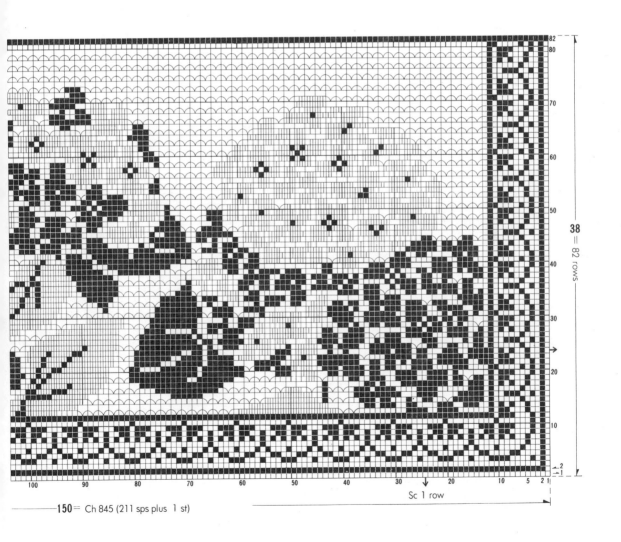

38 = 82 rows

Sc 1 row

150 = Ch 845 (211 sps plus 1 st)

MATERIALS AND EQUIPMENT:
Mercerized crochet cotton, No. 40, white, 50g for Table Center and 120g for one Cushion Cover. Steel crochet hook size 0.90mm. Blue cotton satin, 100cm by 50cm. Kapok, 400g. Cotton cord, 0.3cm in diameter and 180cm long.

FINISHED SIZE: Table Center, 49cm in diameter; Cushion Cover, 46cm in diameter. Width of ruffle, 6cm.

GAUGE: 1 dc = 0.5cm.

DIRECTIONS: FOR TABLE CENTER:
Ch 16, join with sl st to form ring. Rnd 1: (Ch 4, tr 2) cluster, (ch 5, 3-tr cluster) 11 times, ch 2, hdc 1. Rnd 2: (Sc 1, ch 6) 11 times, sc 1, ch 3, hdc 1. Rnds 3-42: Work following chart, making 12 pineapple patterns. Work 3 rnds of edging.

FOR CUSHION COVER: Make inner cushion, 48cm in diameter. Stuff with kapok. Work 42 rnds in same manner as Table Center. Make 2 pieces. With right sides facing, work for ruffle joining front and back pieces. After working half rnd of Rnd 1, insert inner cushion and continue to work for ruffle. Rnds 2-11: Work in ch and sc following chart. Insert cotton cord into open-work of Rnd 42 of front and back.

Ruffle for Cushion Cover

With right sides facing, join front and back together, working first rnd for ruffle.

Attach thread

Cotton Cord
Insert cord into spaces of front and back

58

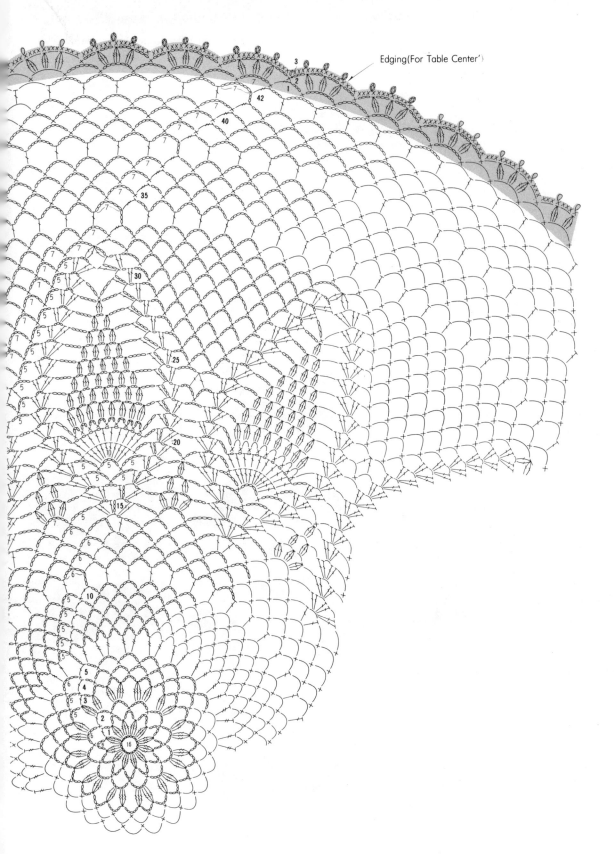

Edging(For Table Center')

59

Butterfly Table Center, shown on page 17.

MATERIALS AND EQUIPMENT: Mercerized crochet cotton, No. 40, 100g white. Steel crochet hook size 1.00mm.
FINISHED SIZE: 66cm in diameter.
GAUGE 10cm = 14.5 sps; 10cm = 14.5 rows.
DIRECTIONS: Rnd 1: Begin at center, ch 12, join with tr to form first sps. Rnd 2: Ch 7, (tr 1, ch 7, tr 1, ch 3) 3 times, tr 1, ch 3. Rnds 3-30: Work in filet crochet following chart and increasing at corners. Rows 31-43: Work in filet crochet following chart and decreasing at each side to complete one side at a time. Attach new thread at each corner of remaining sides and work in same manner. Work 8 rnds of edging.

Chart for Starting and Increasing

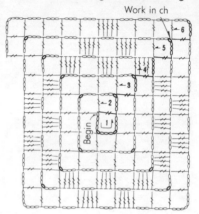

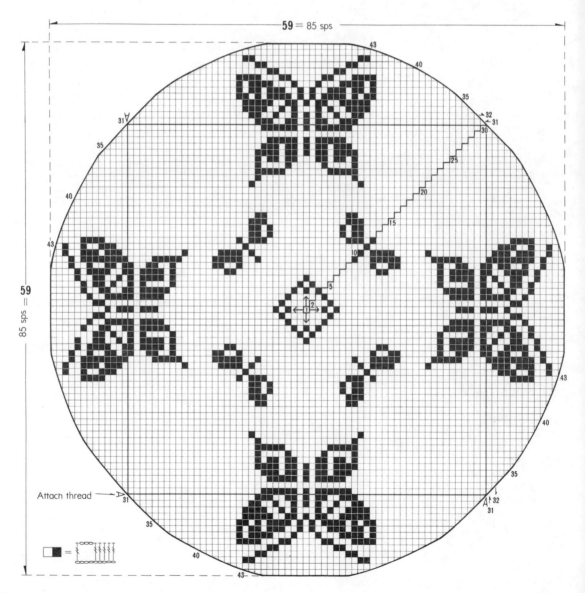

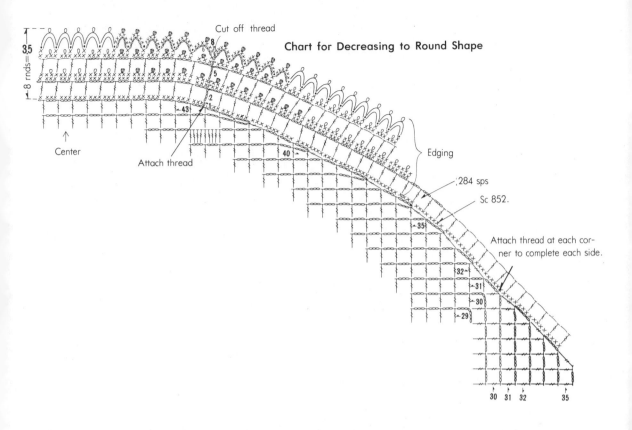

Chart for Decreasing to Round Shape

3.5

8 rnds

Cut off thread

Center

Attach thread

Edging

284 sps

Sc 852.

Attach thread at each corner to complete each side.

30 31 32   35

Diamond-pattern Chair Back, Sofa Back and Matching Cushion Covers, shown on pages 18 & 19.

MATERIALS AND EQUIPMENT:
Mercerized crochet cotton, No. 40, white, 200g for Sofa Back and 90g for one Chair Back. Steel crochet hook size 1.00mm.

FINISHED SIZE: Sofa Back, 115cm by 70cm; Chair Back, 43.5cm by 70cm.

GAUGE: 1 tr = 0.8cm.

DIRECTIONS: FOR SOFA BACK: Ch 477 to make 14 patterns plus 1st. Row 1: Ch 4, {(2-tr, ch 2, 2-tr) cluster, ch 4, (2-tr, ch 2, 2-tr) cluster, ch 3} 14 times, omit last 3-ch, end with tr 1. Rows 2-26: Work following chart. Rows 27-74 Repeat Rows 3-26 twice. Rows 75-86: Work to complete each pattern. Work 2 rnds of edging on sides and bottom. Work 1 row of sc over foundation ch.

FOR CHAIR BACK: Ch 171 to make 5 patterns plus 1 st. Work in same manner as Sofa Back.

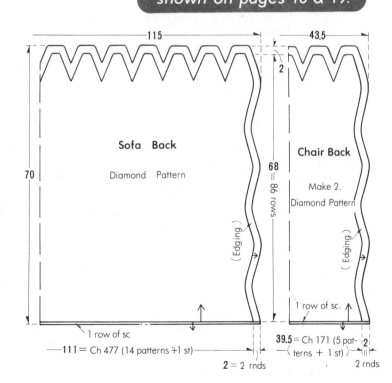

115

43.5

Sofa Back

Diamond Pattern

Chair Back

Make 2.
Diamond Pattern

70

68 = 86 rows

2

(Edging)

(Edging)

1 row of sc.

1 row of sc

111 = Ch 477 (14 patterns + 1 st)

2 = 2 rnds

39.5 = Ch 171 (5 patterns + 1 st)

2

2 rnds

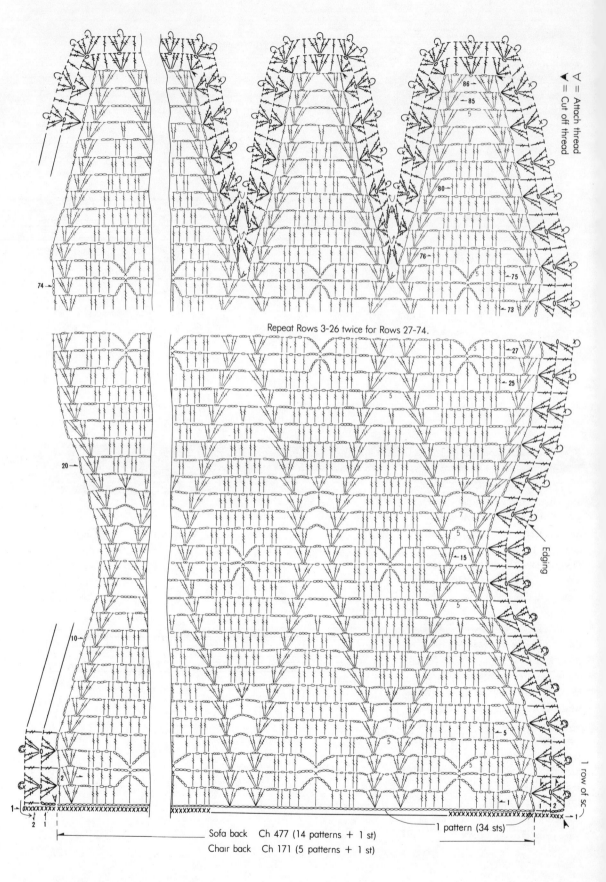

V = Attach thread

▼ = Cut off thread

Repeat Rows 3-26 twice for Rows 27-74.

Edging

1 row of sc

Sofa back   Ch 477 (14 patterns + 1 st)

Chair back   Ch 171 (5 patterns + 1 st)

1 pattern (34 sts)

⟨Matching Cushion Cover⟩

MATERIALS AND EQUIPMENT (FOR ONE): Mercerized crochet cotton, No. 40, 100g white. Steel crochet hook size 1.00mm. Blue (pink) Bemberg, 50cm by 100cm. Kapok, 400g. Blue (pink) satin ribbon, 0.9cm by 250cm.

FINISHED SIZE: 45cm in diameter.

GAUGE: 1 tr = 0.8cm.

DIRECTIONS: Make inner cushion 46cm in diameter with Bemberg and stuff with kapok. Ch 8, join with sl st to form ring. Rnd 1: Ch 4, (ch 1, tr 1) 15 times, ch 1, end with sl st. Rnds 2-28: Work following chart and make 8 diamond patterns. Make second piece in same manner except Rnd 28. Work Rnd 28 joining with first piece. After working half rnd, insert inner cushion and continue to work joining 2 pieces together. Cut ribbon into two. Insert each ribbon between 2 peices and tie ends into bows at each side.

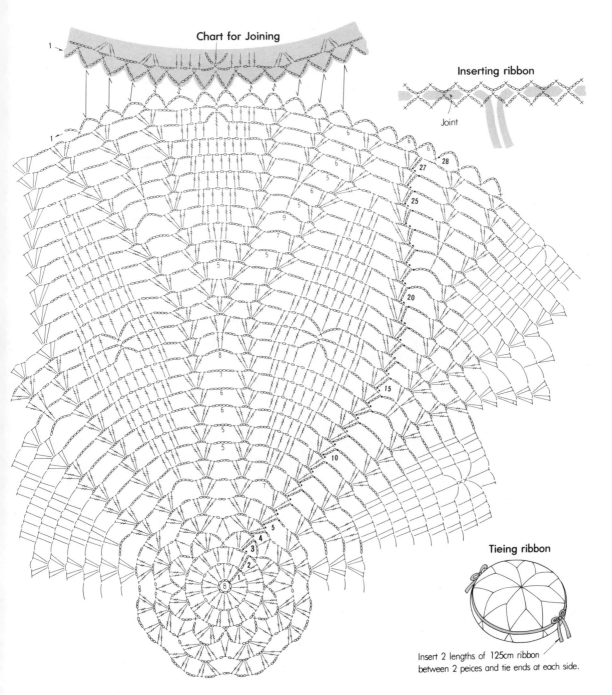

Chart for Joining

Inserting ribbon

Joint

Tieing ribbon

Insert 2 lengths of 125cm ribbon between 2 peices and tie ends at each side.

MATERIALS AND EQUIPMENT: Mercerized crochet cotton, No. 40, 300g white. Steel crochet hook size 0.90mm.

FINISHED SIZE: 131.5cm by 100cm.

GAUGE: 1 tr = 0.7cm.

SIZE OF MOTIF: 10.5cm square.

DIRECTIONS: FOR FIRST MOTIF: Ch 4, join with sl st to form ring. Rnd 1: Ch 4, tr 1, (ch 7, tr 2) 3 times, ch 3, tr 1. Rnds 2-8: Work following chart. **FOR SECOND MOTIF:** Make in same manner as First Motif except Rnd 8. Work Rnd 8 joining with First Motif. Make and join 8 by 11 motifs. Work 10 rnds of edging increasing at corners.

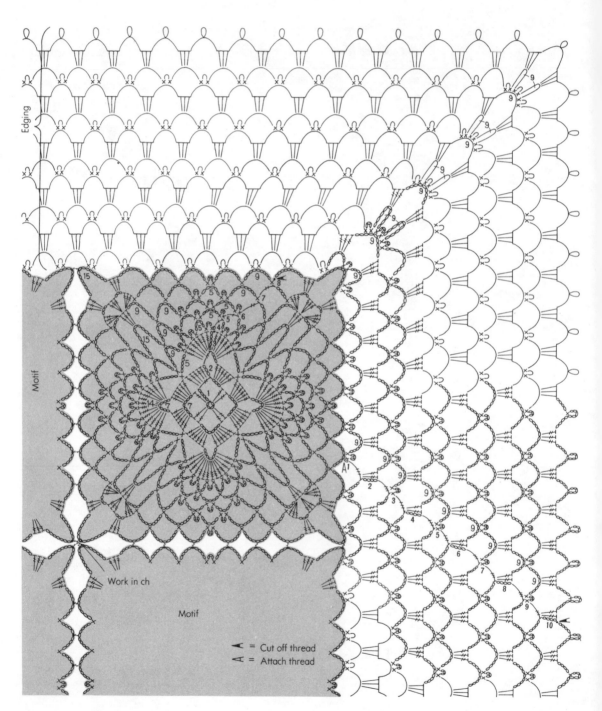

Edging

Motif

Work in ch

Motif

◄ = Cut off thread

◁ = Attach thread

Diagram

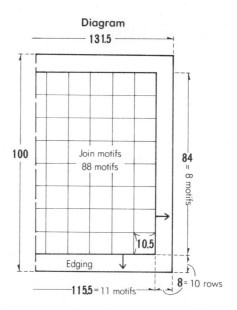

131.5

100

84 = 8 motifs

Join motifs
88 motifs

10.5

Edging

8 = 10 rows

115.5 = 11 motifs

Doily, shown on page 21, top.

MATERIALS AND EQUIPMENT: Mercerized crochet cotton, No. 40, 20g white. Steel crochet hook size 0.90mm. FINISHED SIZE: 28cm in diameter. GAUGE: 1 dc = 0.5cm. DIRECTIONS: Ch 8, join with sl st to form ring. Rnd 1: Ch 3, dc 24 in ring, end with sl st. Rnd 2: Ch 1, (sc 1, ch 3) 23 times, sc 1, ch 1, hdc 1. Rnds 3-8: Work in ch and sc following chart and increasing. Rnd 9: Ch 1, (sc 7 in 1p) 24 times, sl st 3. Rnd 10: (Sc 1, ch 3, 4-ch picot, ch 4, 3-ch picot, ch 3) 24 times, sl st 6. Rnds 11-15: Work in ch with picot and sc following chart and increasing. Rnds 16-23: Work in dc and ch following chart.

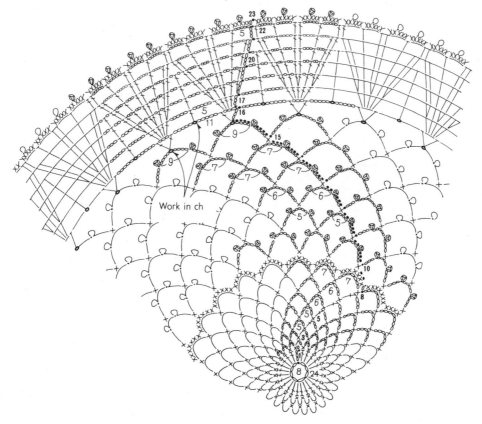

Doily, shown on page 20.

MATERIALS AND EQUIPMENT: Mercerized crochet cotton, No. 70, 20g beige. Steel crochet hook size 0.75mm.
FINISHED SIZE: 34cm in diameter.
GAUGE: 1 dc = 0.4cm.

DIRECTIONS: Ch 8, join with sl st to form ring. Rnd 1: Ch 1, sc 16 in ring end with sl st. Rnd 2: Ch 1, (sc 1, ch 8) 8 times, end with sl st. Rnds 3-41: Work following chart and make 8 patterns.

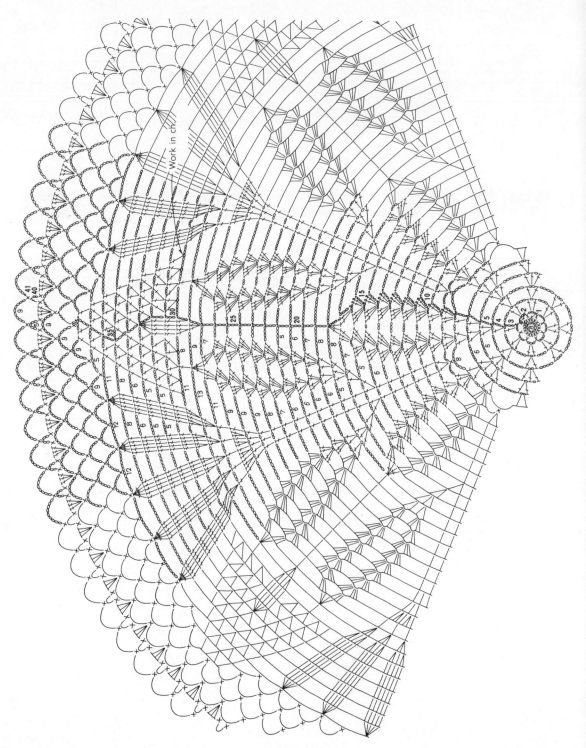

MATERIALS AND EQUIPMENT: Mercerized crochet cotton, No. 40, 25g white. Steel crochet hook size 0.90mm.
FINISHED SIZE: 32cm in diameter.
GAUGE: 1 dc = 0.6cm.

DIRECTIONS: Make 1p at thread end. Rnd 1: Ch 1, sc 6 in 1p. Rnd 2: Ch 1, (sc 1, ch 5) 5 times, sc 1, ch 2, dc 1. Rnds 3-32: Work following chart and make 6 patterns.

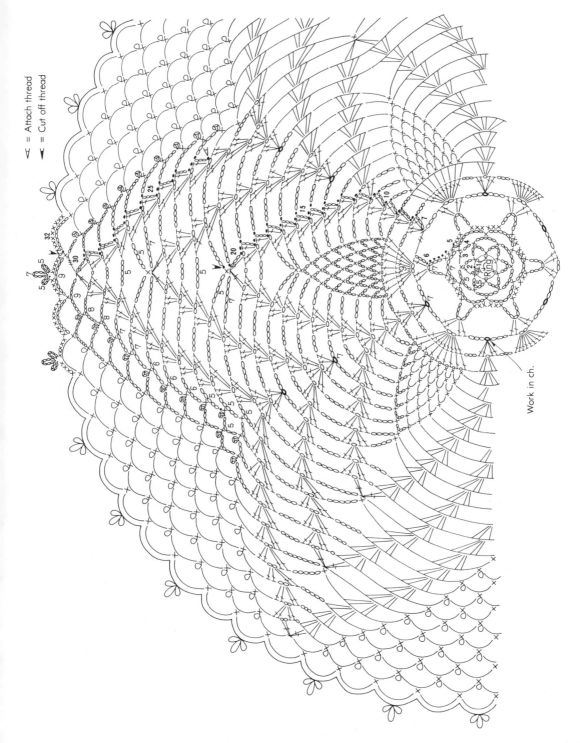

MATERIALS AND EQUIPMENT: Mercerized crochet cotton, No. 40, 20g white. Steel crochet hook size 0.90mm. White linen, 25cm by 21cm. Six-strand embroidery floss, No. 25: Small amount each of pink and light green.
FINISHED SIZE: 31cm by 27cm.
GAUGE: 1 dc = 0.4cm.

DIRECTIONS: FOR MOTIF: Ch 10. Rnd 1: Ch 3, dc 25, end with sl st. Rnd 2: Ch 3, dc 37, end with sl st. Make 10 motifs. Turn back seam allowance of linen and machine-stitch. Buttonhole-stitch over machine-stitch.
Work 3 rnds of edging in filet crochet all around. Cut off thread. Attach new thread as indicated and work Rows 4 & 5 at each side. Attach thread again and work Rnd 6, joining motifs with edging. Work Rnd 8 to finish. Embroider on each motif.

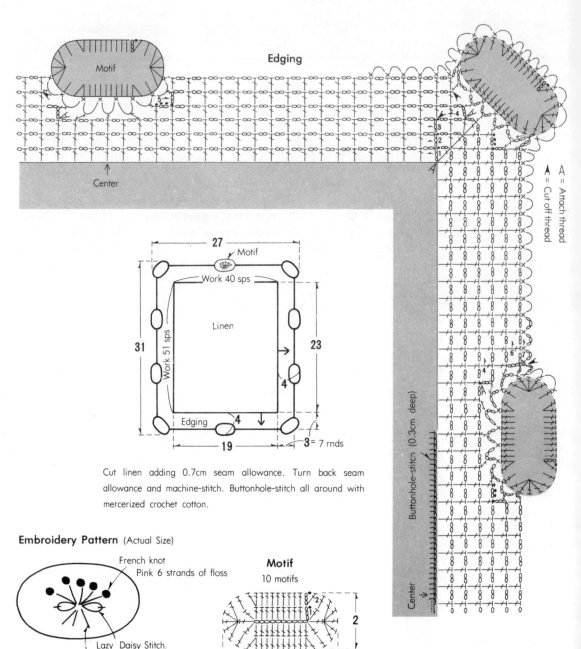

Cut linen adding 0.7cm seam allowance. Turn back seam allowance and machine-stitch. Buttonhole-stitch all around with mercerized crochet cotton.

Embroidery Pattern (Actual Size)

French knot
Pink 6 strands of floss
Lazy Daisy Stitch
Straight Stitch
Light green
3 strands of floss

Motif
10 motifs

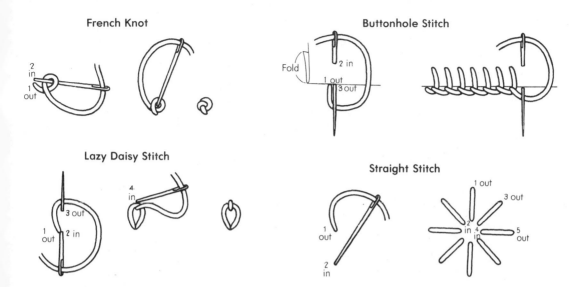

French Knot

Buttonhole Stitch

Lazy Daisy Stitch

Straight Stitch

Tablecloth, shown on pages 24 & 25.

MATERIALS AND EQUIPMENT: Mercerized crochet cotton, No. 40, 180g white. Steel crochet hook size 0.90mm. White linen, 112cm square.

FINISHED SIZE: 113cm square.

GAUGE: 10cm = 17,5 sps; 10cm = 18 rows.

DIRECTIONS: FOR LARGE MOTIF: Ch 28 to make 9 bls plus 1 st. Row 1: Ch 3, dc 28 in ch, ch 6. Row 2: Ch 3, dc 9 (ch 2, dc 1) 7 times, dc 3, dc 6 adding foundation ch (see details below), ch 6. Rows 3-34: Work following chart. Work 1 rnd of edging. Make 11 large motifs.

FOR SMALL MOTIF: Make required number of small motifs following chart. Cut out linen adding 0.5cm seam allowance. Turn back seam allowance and machine-stitch. Work 3 rnds of edging around linen. Sew on large and small motifs as shown in diagram.

Diagram.

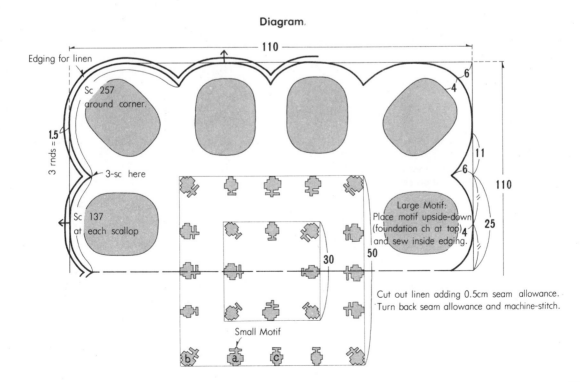

Edging for linen

Sc 257 around corner.

3-sc here

Sc 137 at each scallop

3 rnds = 1.5

110

6

4

11

6

110

25

Large Motif: Place motif upside-down (foundation ch at top) and sew inside edging.

30

50

4

Small Motif

Cut out linen adding 0.5cm seam allowance. Turn back seam allowance and machine-stitch.

b   a   c

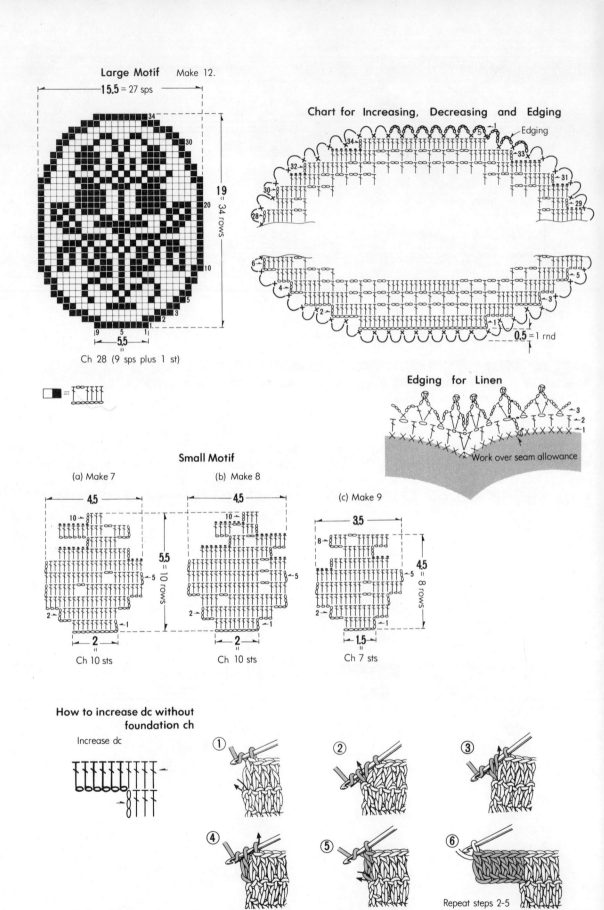

Large Motif   Make 12.

15.5 = 27 sps

19 = 34 rows

5.5

Ch 28 (9 sps plus 1 st)

Chart for Increasing, Decreasing and Edging

Edging

0.5 = 1 rnd

Edging for Linen

Work over seam allowance

Small Motif

(a) Make 7

(b) Make 8

(c) Make 9

4.5

5.5 = 10 rows

Ch 10 sts

4.5

Ch 10 sts

3.5

4.5 = 8 rows

1.5

Ch 7 sts

How to increase dc without foundation ch

Increase dc

① ② ③

④ ⑤ ⑥

Repeat steps 2-5

MATERIALS AND EQUIPMENT: Mercerized crochet cotton, No. 50, 15g white. Steel crochet hook size 0.75mm.

FINISHED SIZE: Neck, 40cm. Width, 7.5cm.

GAUGE: 1 dc = 0.3cm.

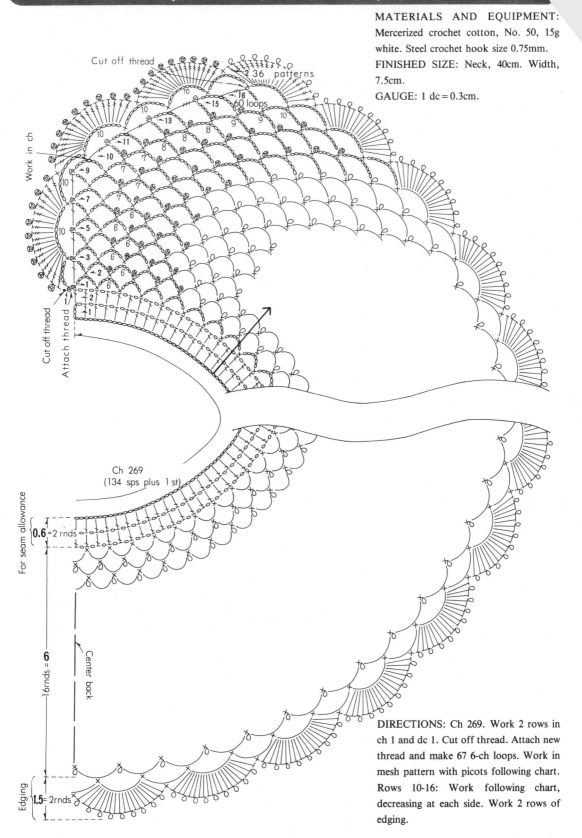

Cut off thread

36 patterns

60 loops

Work in ch

Cut off thread

Attach thread

Ch 269
(134 sps plus 1 st)

For seam allowance

0.6 = 2 rnds

16 rnds = 6

Center back

Edging

1.5 = 2 rnds

DIRECTIONS: Ch 269. Work 2 rows in ch 1 and dc 1. Cut off thread. Attach new thread and make 67 6-ch loops. Work in mesh pattern with picots following chart. Rows 10-16: Work following chart, decreasing at each side. Work 2 rows of edging.

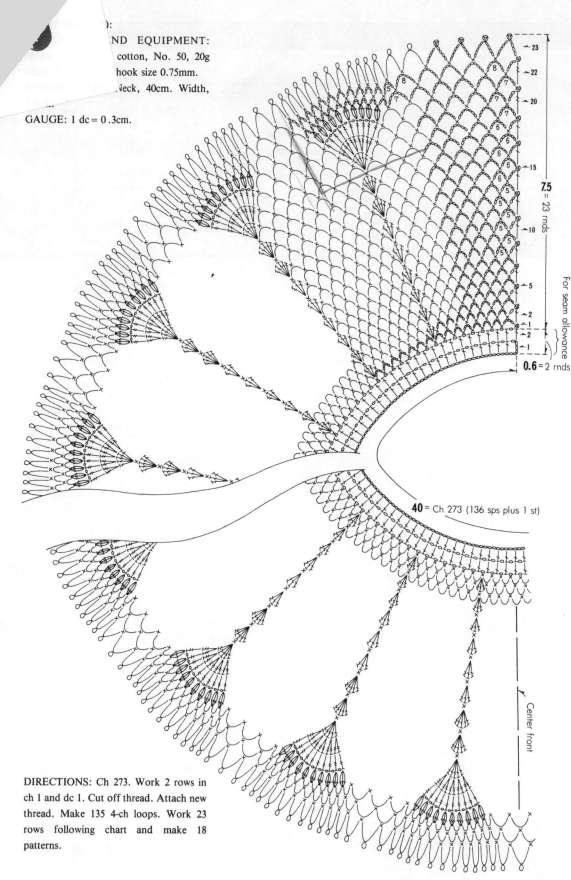

D):

ND EQUIPMENT:
cotton, No. 50, 20g
hook size 0.75mm.
Neck, 40cm. Width,

GAUGE: 1 dc = 0.3cm.

7.5 = 23 rnds

For seam allowance

0.6 = 2 rnds

40 = Ch 273 (136 sps plus 1 st)

Center front

DIRECTIONS: Ch 273. Work 2 rows in ch 1 and dc 1. Cut off thread. Attach new thread. Make 135 4-ch loops. Work 23 rows following chart and make 18 patterns.

(C) MATERIALS AND EQUIPMENT: Mercerized crochet cotton, No. 70, 10g white. Steel crochet hook size 0.60mm.

FINISHED SIZE: Width, 4cm. Length, 92.5cm.

GAUGE: 2.3cm = 7 sps; 10cm = 26 rows.

DIRECTIONS: Ch 22. Work in filet crochet following chart. Repeat Rows 1-6 40 times to make 240 rows. Work 2 rnds of edging. On 2nd rnd, work sc 1 in each st but sc 3 in each 2-ch bar between first tr to last tr (7 2-ch bars) of each curve.

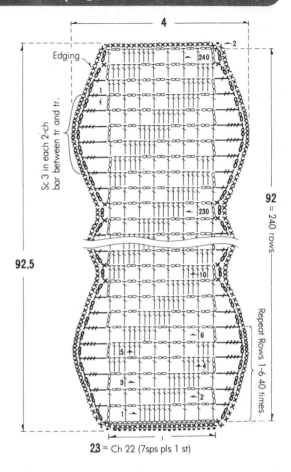

(D) MATERIALS AND EQUIPMENT: Mercerized crochet cotton, No. 70, 20g white. Steel crochet hook size 0.60mm.

FINISHED SIZE: Width, 6.5cm. Length, 101cm.

GAUGE: 4.5cm = 14 sps; 10cm = 25 rows.

DIRECTIONS: Ch 43. Work in filet crochet following chart. Repeat Rows 1-11 23 times to make 253 rows. Inc and dec on left side. Attach thread and work (tr tr 1, ch 2) to end.

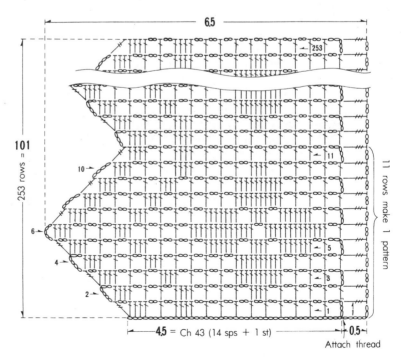

73

(E) MATERIALS AND EQUIPMENT: Mercerized crochet cotton, No. 70, 10g white. Steel crochet hook size 0.60mm. FINISHED SIZE: Width, 3cm. Length, 97.5cm. GAUGE: 2cm = 7 sps; 10cm = 22 rows. DIRECTIONS: Ch 22. Following chart, work in filet crochet making 5-dc popcorns as shown. Repeat Rows 1-10 up to Row 212. Work sc all around on 1st rnd of edging. On 2nd rnd, work in shell-pattern (dc 6, sc 1) all around. Dc 7 at corners instead of dc 6.

(F) MATERIALS AND EQUIPMENT: Mercerized crochet cotton, No. 70, 10g white. Steel crochet hook size 0.60mm. FINISHED SIZE: Width, 2.5cm. Length, 92cm. GAUGE: 1 dc = 0.4cm; 1 pattern (14 rows) = 4 cm. DIRECTIONS: Ch 10, end with sl st to form ring. Row 1: Ch 3, dc 12 in ring. Row 2: Ch 3, (ch 1, dc 1) 12 times. Rows 3-14: Following chart, work in ch 5 and sc 1 to form pineapple pattern. Repeat Rows 1-14 23 times up to Row 322.

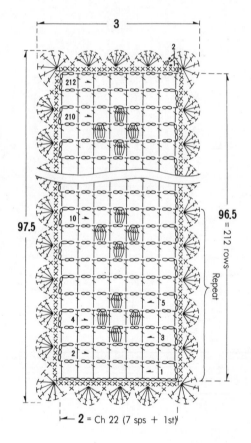

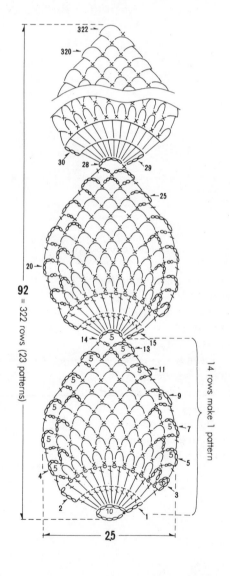

(G) MATERIALS AND EQUIPMENT: Mercerized crochet cotton, No. 70, 10g white. Steel crochet hook size 0.60mm.
FINISHED SIZE: Width, 5cm. Length, 103.5cm.
GAUGE: 4.5 cm = 14 sps; 10cm = 25 rows.
DIRECTIONS: Ch 43. Work in filet crochet following chart. Repeat Rows 1-24 up to Row 257. Work sc all around on 1st rnd of edging. On 2nd rnd, work in sl st and 5-ch picot.

Edging

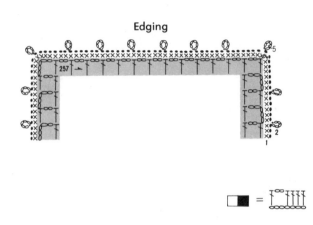

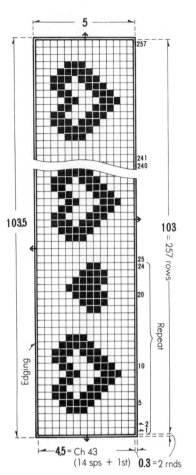

Doily, shown on page 29.

MATERIALS AND EQUIPMENT: Mercerized crochet cotton, No. 40, 10g blue. Steel crochet hook size 0.90mm.
Blue linen, 41cm by 18cm.
FINISHED SIZE: 45cm by 22.5cm.
GAUGE: 1 dc = 0.5cm.

DIRECTIONS: To make Motif, make 1p at thread end. Ch 1, (sc 1, ch 4, 2-tr, ch 4) 4 times, end with sl st. Cut off thread. Make 44 motifs. Cut out oval from blue linen. Turn back seam allowance and machine-stitch. Buttonhole-stitch. Work in filet crochet picking up sts from buttonhole sts. On 2nd rnd, join motifs with edging.

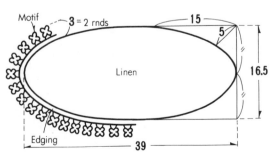

※ Cut out oval from blue linen, adding 0.7cm seam allowance. Turn back seam allowance and machine-stitch. Buttonhole-stitch all around with mercerized crochet cotton (see page 69).

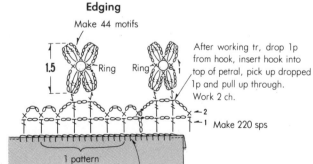

Tissue Case, shown on page 29.

MATERIALS AND EQUIPMENT: Mercerized crochet cotton, No. 40, small amount of soft pink. Steel crochet hook size 0.90mm. Soft pink linen, 21cm by 13cm.
FINISHED SIZE: See diagram.
DIRECTIONS: 1. Cut out front and back adding 0.7cm seam allowance. Turn back seam allowance of front opening and machine-stitch. 2. With right sides facing, sew front and back together leaving top open, Turn inside out. 3. Buttonhole-stitch all around, working on front piece only except top edge of back. Buttonhole-stitch top edge of back. 4. Make 4 motifs. To make motif, make 1p at thread end. Rnd 1: Ch 1, sc 16 in 1p, end with sl st. Rnd 2: Ch 1, (sc 1, ch 4, 3-tr, ch 4) 4 times, end with sl st. Sew 3 motifs onto front. 5. Following chart, work 4 rows of edging (a) for front opening, joining motif. 6. Work 2 rnds of edging (b) for front and back opening. Work 2 rnds of edging (c) for three sides.

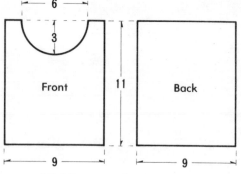

Add 0.7cm seam allowance

Chart for Motif and Edging

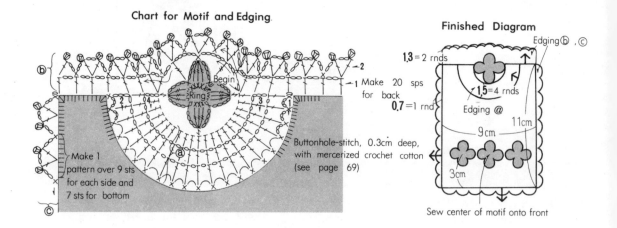

Finished Diagram

Cosmetic Case, shown on page 29.

MATERIALS AND EQUIPMENT: Mercerized crochet cotton, No. 40, small amount of soft pink. Steel crochet hook size 0.90mm. Soft pink linen, 34cm by 18cm. Unbleached linen, 16cm by 12cm. Soft pink cotton fabric, 34cm by 18cm.
FINISHED SIZE: Width, 16cm. Depth, 11cm.
DIRECTIONS: 1. Cut out 1 piece each from linen (soft pink and unbleached) and cotton fabric adding 0.7cm seam allowance. Turn back seam allowance of front patch and machine-stitch. 2. Make 4 motifs (work same as motifs for

tissue case). 3. Buttonhole-stitch around front patch. Following chart, work 3 rnds of edging, joining with one motif. 4. Place patch on front matching centers and slip-stitch along buttonhole stitches. 5. Fold linen and cotton fabric as shown on next page and sew two pieces together with right sides facing. 6. Turn inside out from opening. Slip-stitch edges of opening. 7. Buttonhole-stitch on three sides of flap, catching linen only. Work 3 rows of edging over buttonhole stitches. Sew 3 motifs onto front patch.

76

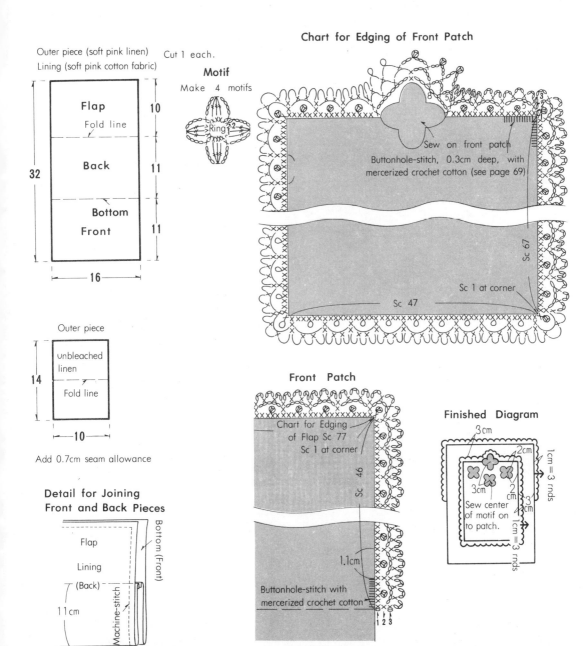

Outer piece (soft pink linen)
Lining (soft pink cotton fabric)

Cut 1 each.

Motif
Make 4 motifs

Flap 10
Fold line

Back 11

32

Bottom
Front 11

16

Chart for Edging of Front Patch

Sew on front patch
Buttonhole-stitch, 0.3cm deep, with
mercerized crochet cotton (see page 69)

Sc 67
Sc 1 at corner
Sc 47

Outer piece

unbleached
linen
Fold line

14

10

Add 0.7cm seam allowance

**Detail for Joining
Front and Back Pieces**

Flap
Lining
(Back)
11 cm
Machine-stitch
Bottom (Front)

Front Patch

Chart for Edging
of Flap Sc 77
Sc 1 at corner

Sc 46

1.1cm

Buttonhole-stitch with
mercerized crochet cotton

1 2 3

Finished Diagram

3cm
2cm
1cm = 3 rnds
3cm 2cm
3cm
Sew center
of motif on
to patch.
1cm = 3 rnds
1cm = 3 rnds

Compact Case, shown on page 29.

MATERIALS AND EQUIPMENT: Mercerized crochet cotton, No. 40, small amount of soft pink. Steel crochet hook size 0.90mm. Soft pink linen, 17cm by 10cm. Polyester fiberfill.

FINISHED SIZE: 10cm in diameter.

GAUGE: 1 dc = 0.5cm.

DIRECTIONS: 1. Cut out front, 5.5cm in diameter, and back, 8.5cm in diameter, adding seam allowance. Turn back seam allowance and machine-stitch. Buttonhole-stitch all around. Work same as Back. 2. Work 3 rnds of edging around Front. 3. With wrong sides facing, join front and back together working 2 rnds of edging and leaving top edges open. Work edging for front and back opening individually. 4. Center motif on front and sew on. 5. Make button following chart, stuff with fiberfill and sew on. 6. Make 3cm-cord in ch and sc for button loop. Sew on back.

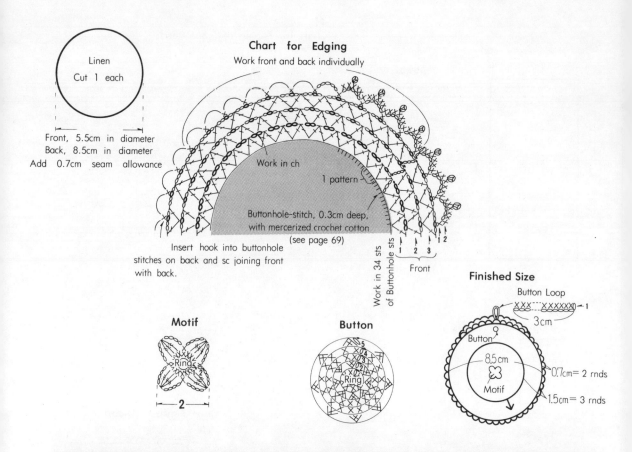

Linen

Cut 1 each

Front, 5.5cm in diameter
Back, 8.5cm in diameter
Add 0.7cm seam allowance

Chart for Edging
Work front and back individually

Work in ch

1 pattern

Buttonhole-stitch, 0.3cm deep,
with mercerized crochet cotton
(see page 69)

Insert hook into buttonhole
stitches on back and sc joining front
with back.

Work in 34 sts of Buttonhole sts

Front

Finished Size

Button Loop

3cm

Button

8.5cm

Motif

0.7cm= 2 rnds

1.5cm= 3 rnds

Motif

Ring

2

Button

Ring

Bedspread, shown on page 23.

MATERIALS AND EQUIPMENT:
Mercerized crochet cotton, No. 40, 1000g
white. Steel crochet hook size 0.90mm.
FINISHED SIZE: 208cm by 166.5cm.
GAUGE: 10cm = 21 rows.
SIZE OF MOTIFS: A & B, 50cm by 48cm. C,
50cm by 31cm. D & D', 32.5cm by 48cm. E &
E', 32.5cm by 31cm.
DIRECTIONS: Ch 301 each for Motifs A, B
and C. Work in filet crochet following chart.
Make 3 motifs each for A and B. Make 4
motifs for C. Ch 196 each for Motifs D and E.
Make 3 motifs each for D and D', and 2 each
for Motifs E and E'. Following diagram, join
motifs working 1 rnd of edging around each
motif.

Diagram

Direction of letters indicates that of motifs.

E´	C	C 50 31	E 32.5 31
D´	B	A 50 0.5 48	D 32.5 48
D´	A	(Join motifs) B 50 48	D
D´	B	A	D
E´	C	C	E´

208 = 5 motifs

166.5 = 4 motifs

Motif A Make 3 motifs

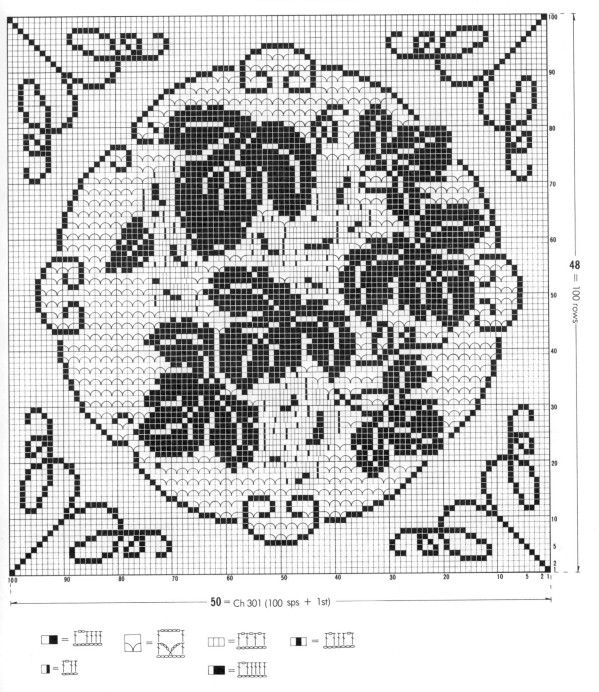

48 = 100 rows

50 = Ch 301 (100 sps + 1 st)

Motif C Make 4 motifs

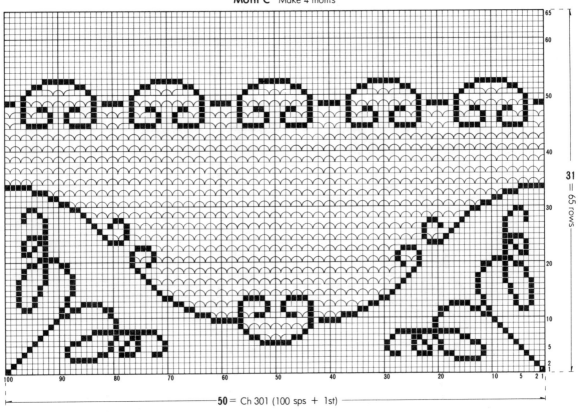

65
60
50
40
31 = 65 rows
30
20
10
5
2
1

100 90 80 70 60 50 40 30 20 10 5 2 1

50 = Ch 301 (100 sps + 1st)

Motifs E, E' Make 2 motifs each
※ Reverse pattern for E'

How to join motifs

Cut off thread   Attach thread

Attach thread

Cut off thread

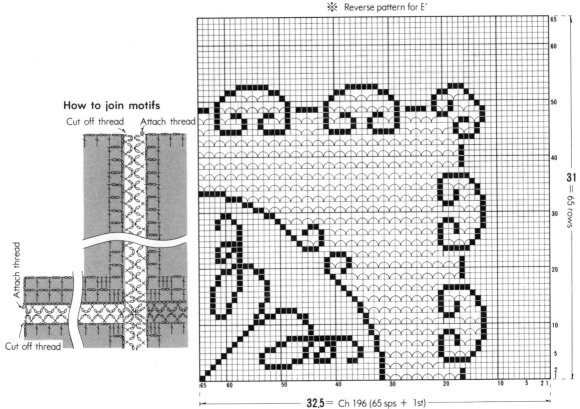

65
60
50
40
31 = 65 rows
30
20
10
5
2
1

65 60 50 40 30 20 10 5 2 1

32.5 = Ch 196 (65 sps + 1st)

Motifs D, D' Make 3 motifs each

※ Reverse pattern for D'

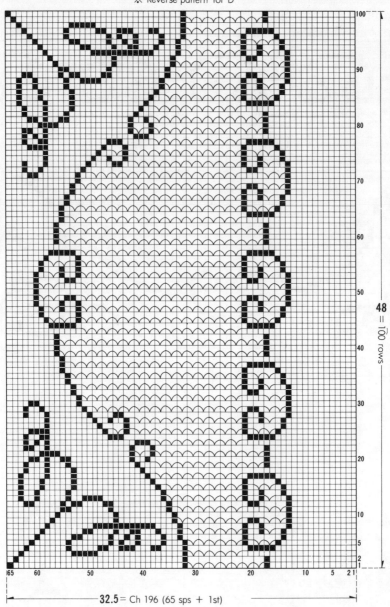

48 = 100 rows

32.5 = Ch 196 (65 sps + 1st)

Bedspread, shown on page 30.

MATERIALS AND EQUIPMENT; Mercerized crochet cotton, No. 40, 150g white. Steel crochet hook size 0.90mm. Powder green sheeting, 98cm by 610cm. Cotton fabric for lining, 90cm by 540cm.

GAUGE: 11 dc = 5cm (motif); 9 sps = 4cm; 10cm = 18 rows.

FINISHED SIZE: 274cm by 182cm.

DIRECTIONS: To make motif, make 1p at thread end. Ch 3, dc 15 in 1p. Work following chart and form star shape. Make 4 different sizes of motifs. Work in filet crochet for tapes A to G following charts on page 84. Make pineapples for tapes H to N. Lightly starch finished motifs and tapes and press tapes into curves as shown. Place motifs and tapes on center rectangle and machine-stitch all around edges of each peice. Use 2 rows of tape ends on each side for seam allowance when joining with borders. Join center rectangle with borders. With wrong sides facing, bind edges of top and lining together with fabrics (a) and (b).

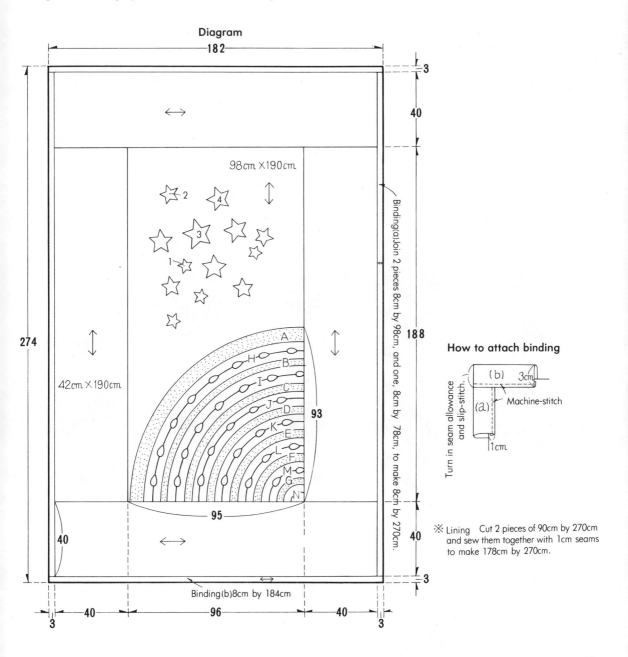

Diagram

How to attach binding

※ Lining   Cut 2 pieces of 90cm by 270cm and sew them together with 1cm seams to make 178cm by 270cm.

Tape

A

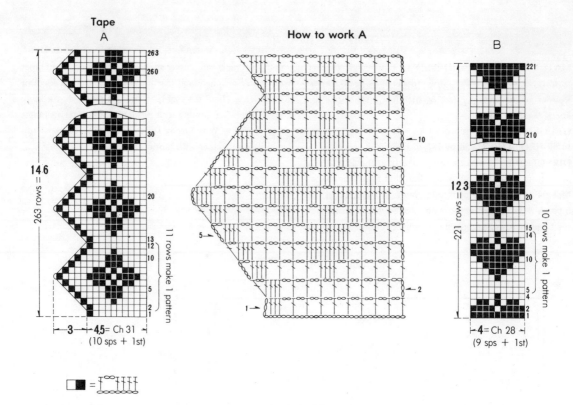

How to work A

263 rows = 146

11 rows make 1 pattern

3 — 4.5 = Ch 31
(10 sps + 1st)

B

221 rows = 123

10 rows make 1 pattern

4 = Ch 28
(9 sps + 1st)

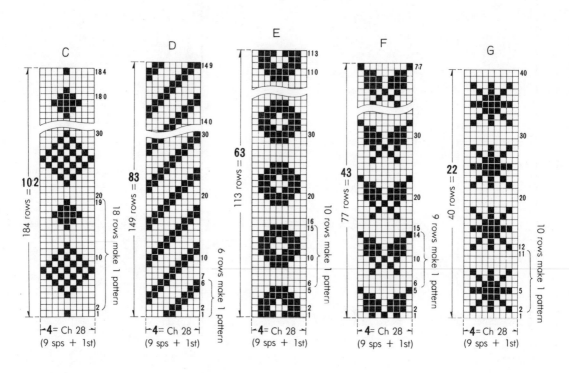

C

184 rows = 102

18 rows make 1 pattern

4 = Ch 28
(9 sps + 1st)

D

149 rows = 83

6 rows make 1 pattern

4 = Ch 28
(9 sps + 1st)

E

113 rows = 63

10 rows make 1 pattern

4 = Ch 28
(9 sps + 1st)

F

77 rows = 43

9 rows make 1 pattern

4 = Ch 28
(9 sps + 1st)

G

70 rows = 22

10 rows make 1 pattern

4 = Ch 28
(9 sps + 1st)

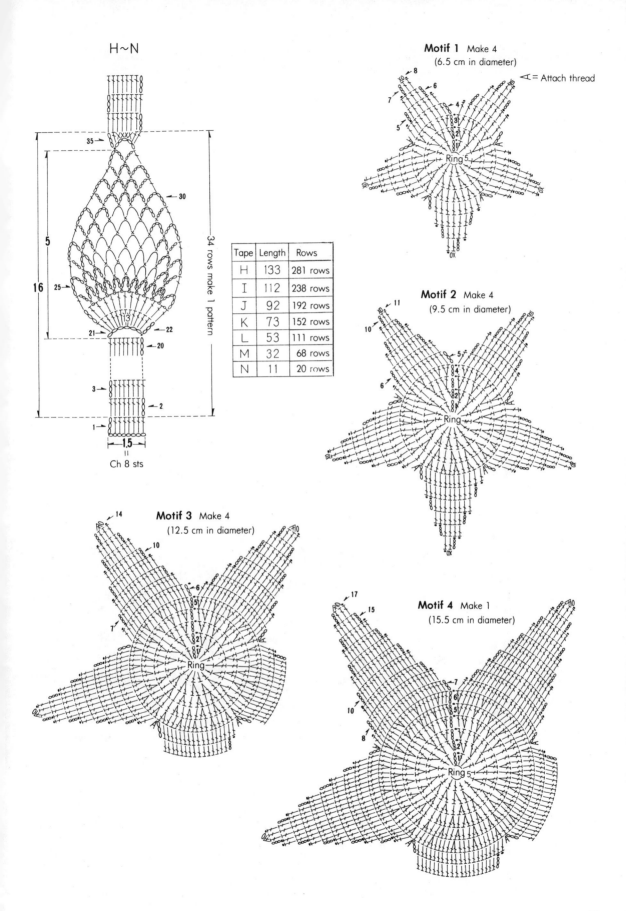

H~N

Tape	Length	Rows
H	133	281 rows
I	112	238 rows
J	92	192 rows
K	73	152 rows
L	53	111 rows
M	32	68 rows
N	11	20 rows

Ch 8 sts

Motif 1 Make 4
(6.5 cm in diameter)

⊰ = Attach thread

Motif 2 Make 4
(9.5 cm in diameter)

Motif 3 Make 4
(12.5 cm in diameter)

Motif 4 Make 1
(15.5 cm in diameter)

MATERIALS AND EQUIPMENT; Mercerized crochet cotton, No. 40, 250g white. Steel crochet hook size 0.90mm.

FINISHED SIZE: 120cm by 34cm.

GAUGE: 10cm = 19.5 sps; 10cm = 19.5 rows.

DIRECTIONS: Ch 112 to make 37 sps plus 1 st. Work in filet crochet following chart and increasing up to Row 27. Work even from Row 28 to Row 235 following chart. Make second piece reversing pattern.

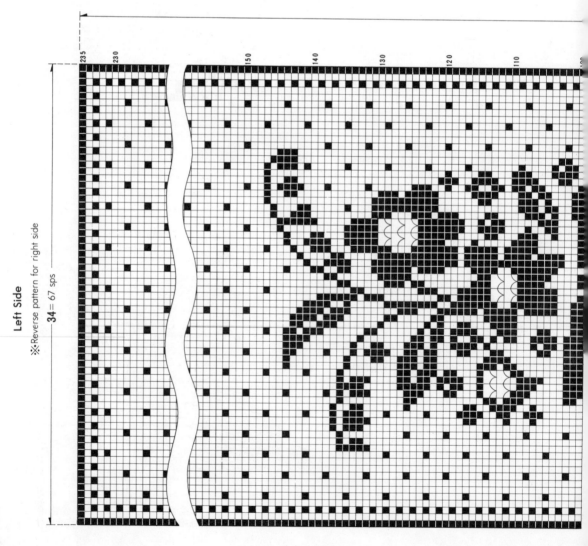

Left Side

※Reverse pattern for right side

34 = 67 sps

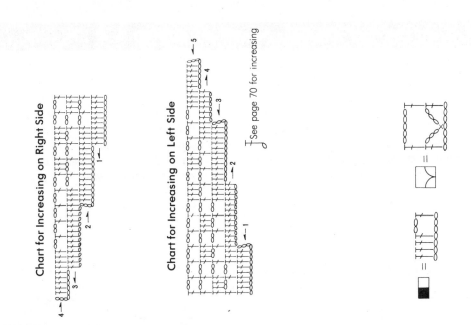

Chart for Increasing on Right Side

Chart for Increasing on Left Side

See page 70 for increasing

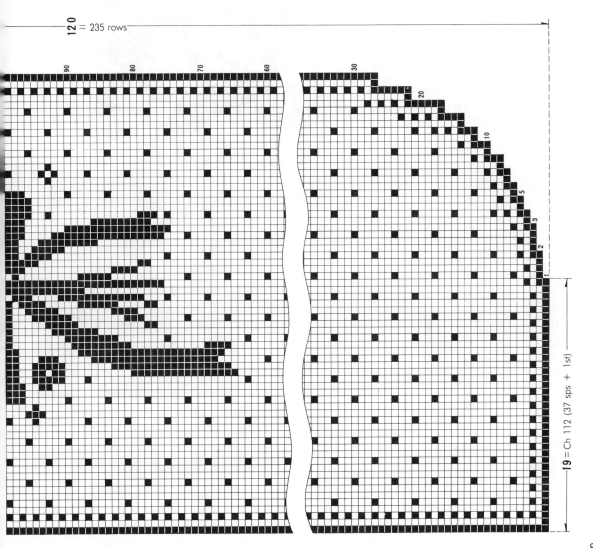

12 0 = 235 rows

19 = Ch 112 (37 sps + 1st)

(A, B, E)

MATERIALS AND EQUIPMENT FOR ONE: Mercerized crochet cotton, No. 40, 40g white. Steel crochet hook size 0.90mm. Cotton fabric: Purple for A, pink for B, blue for E, 90cm by 60cm each. White satin ribbon, 1.4cm by 50cm. 36cm zipper. 43cm-square inner pillow stuffed with kapok. FINISHED SIZE: 40cm square. Width of ruffle, 5.5cm. GAUGE: 10cm = 20 sps; 10cm = 16 rows.

DIRECTIONS: Ch 121 to make 40 sps plus 1 st. Work in filet crochet for 30 rows following chart. Work 1 rnd of edging. Cut fabric as indicated. Sew zipper onto back. Join 3 pieces of ruffle to form ring. With right sides facing and gathered ruffle in between, sew front and back together. Turn inside out. Sew crocheted lace on front. Sew bow in place. Insert inner pillow.

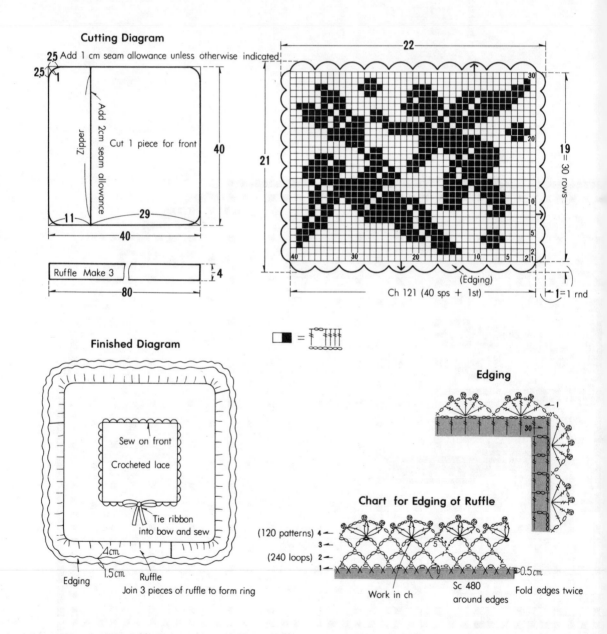

Cutting Diagram

Add 1 cm seam allowance unless otherwise indicated

Cut 1 piece for front

Zipper

Add 2cm seam allowance

Ruffle Make 3

Finished Diagram

Sew on front

Crocheted lace

Tie ribbon into bow and sew

Edging · Ruffle

1.5cm · 4cm

Join 3 pieces of ruffle to form ring

(Edging) · Ch 121 (40 sps + 1st) · 1 = 1 rnd

Edging

Chart for Edging of Ruffle

(120 patterns) 4
3
(240 loops) 2
1

Work in ch · Sc 480 around edges · Fold edges twice · 0.5cm

(C)

MATERIALS AND EQUIPMENT: Mercerized crochet cotton, No. 40, 40g white. Steel crochet hook size 0.90mm. Blue cotton fabric, 90cm by 50cm. White cotton lace edging, 6.5cm by 260cm. 36cm zipper. 43cm-square inner pillow stuffed with kapok.

FINISHED SIZE: 42cm square. Width of ruffle, 5.5cm.

GAUGE: 1 tr = 0.7cm.

DIRECTIONS: FOR FLOWER MOTIF: Make 1p at thread end. Rnd 1: Ch 4 (count 1 tr), (ch 16, sl st 16, tr 4) 6 times, end with sl st. Rnd 2: Sl st 1, *(dc 3, tr 12, dc 1, hdc 1), repeat from * on both sides of each petal, working sc 1 on top and sl st 1 between petals. Cut off thread. Make 6 flowers.

FOR BUD MOTIF: Ch 13 and sl st 12 for stem. Row 1: Ch 4, 6-tr tog. Rnd 2: Ch 4, (tr 1, ch 13, sl st 12, tr 2) 3 times. Rnd 3: Dc 3, * (tr 8, dc 1, hdc 1), repeat from * on both sides of each petal working sc 1 on top and sl st 1 between petals. Make 4 Bud Motifs.

FOR LEAF MOTIF: Following chart, make 6 single-leaf motifs and 5 triple-leaf motifs in same manner as Bud Motif. Cut fabric. Sew zipper onto back. With right sides facing and gathered lace in between, sew front and back together. Turn inside out. Sew flowers, buds and leaves on front. Insert inner pillow.

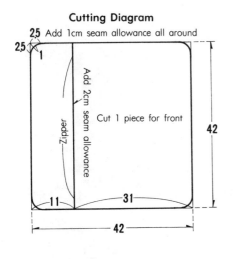

Cutting Diagram

Add 1cm seam allowance all around

Finished Diagram

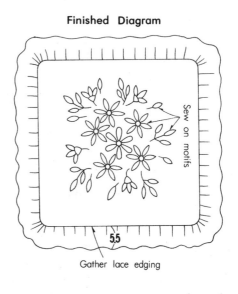

Gather lace edging

Flower Make 6

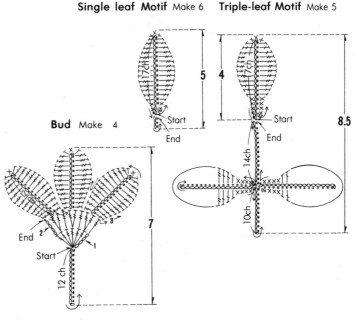

Single leaf Motif Make 6   **Triple-leaf Motif** Make 5

Bud Make 4

(D)

MATERIALS AND EQUIPMENT: Mercerized crochet cotton, No. 40, 30g white. Steel crochet hook size 0.90mm. Pink linen, 80cm by 55cm. White cotton lace edging, 6.5cm by 490cm. Pink grosgrain ribbon, 0.8cm by 236cm. 32cm zipper. Inner pillow stuffed with kapok, 50cm by 40cm.
GAUGE: 5cm = 10 sps; 10cm = 14.5 rows.
FINISHED SIZE: 48cm by 37cm. Width of ruffle, 5cm.

DIRECTIONS: To make tape, ch 43, work 53 rows in filet crochet following chart. Make 2 pieces. Cut fabric. Place crocheted tape on front and gathered lace edging on both sides of tape. Place grosgrain ribbon on tape and lace edging. Machine-stitch on both sides of ribbon. Sew zipper onto back. With right sides facing and gathered lace edging in between, sew front and back together. Turn inside out. Insert inner pillow.

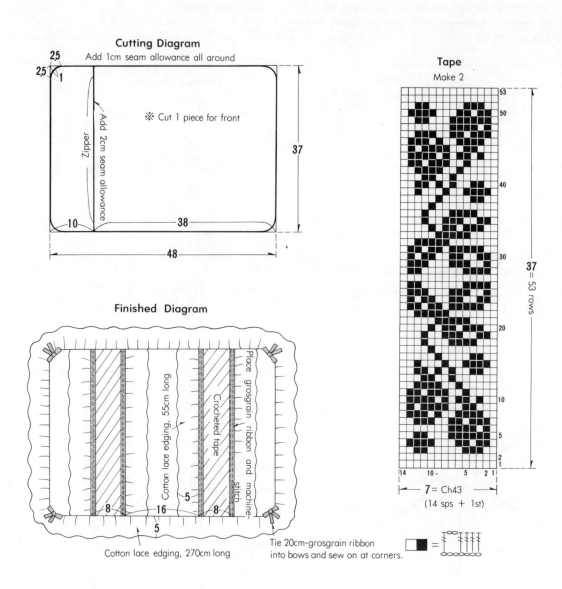

Cutting Diagram
Add 1cm seam allowance all around

2.5
2.5 — 1
Zipper
Add 2cm seam allowance
※ Cut 1 piece for front
37
10
38
48

Tape
Make 2

53
50
40
30
20
10
5
2
1

37 = 53 rows

14   10   5   2 1
7 = Ch43
(14 sps + 1st)

Finished Diagram

Place grosgrain ribbon and machine-stitch
Cotton lace edging, 55cm long
Crocheted tape
8   16   8
5
5
Cotton lace edging, 270cm long
Tie 20cm-grosgrain ribbon into bows and sew on at corners.

90

To Begin

❈ Make chain and form ring.

❈ Make loop.

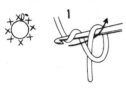

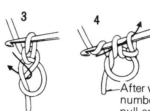
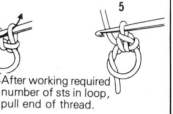

After working required number of sts in loop, pull end of thread.

❈ To pick up sts through chain.

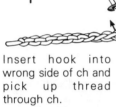
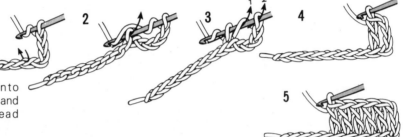

Insert hook into wrong side of ch and pick up thread through ch.

Difference in Stitch Symbols

Note difference in stitch symbols for (a) and (b).

For (a), all sts are worked over chain loop.

For (b), all sts are inserted into ch.

Starting or Turning Chain

On every row or round, st starting or turning a chain is counted as one st except when sc. The stitch symbols at right show one ch st. Sc is equal to one ch, hdc to 2 ch, dc to 3 ch, and so on. When working round, end with sl st in top of starting ch of the rnd and start ch again for next rnd.

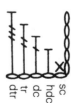

HOW TO INC OR DEC IN FILET CROCHET

TO INCREASE

A

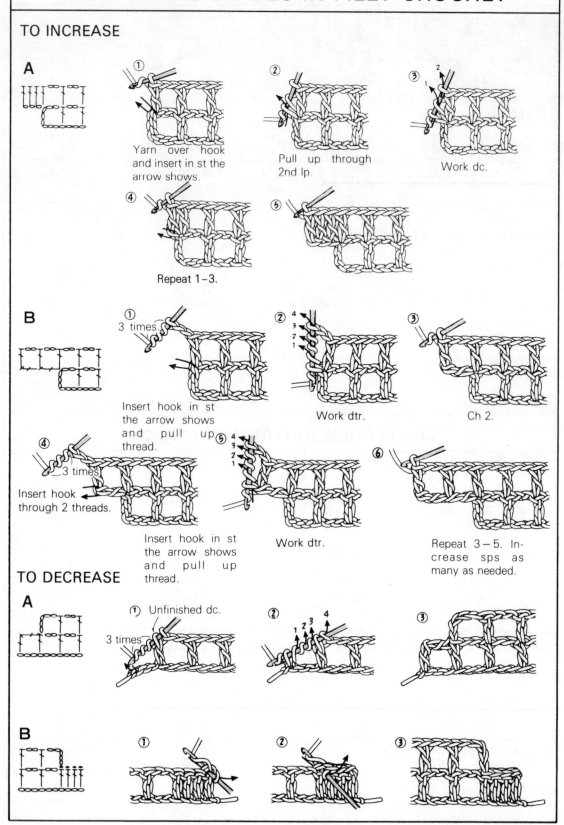

① Yarn over hook and insert in st the arrow shows.

② Pull up through 2nd lp.

③ Work dc.

④ ⑤ Repeat 1–3.

B

① 3 times. Insert hook in st the arrow shows and pull up thread.

② Work dtr.

③ Ch 2.

④ 3 times. Insert hook through 2 threads. Insert hook in st the arrow shows and pull up thread.

⑤ Work dtr.

⑥ Repeat 3 – 5. Increase sps as many as needed.

TO DECREASE

A

① Unfinished dc. 3 times.

②

③

B

①

②

③

92

HOW TO JOIN MOTIFS

A: Join with drawn-out thread.

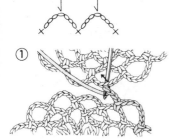

①

Drop lp from hook. Insert hook in sp of net, pick up dropped lp, and pull up through net.

②

Continue working in ch.

③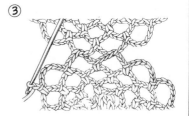

B: Join with sl st.

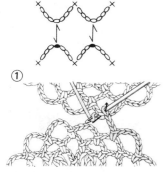

①

Insert hook in net.
Pull up thread through net.

②

③

C: Join with sc.

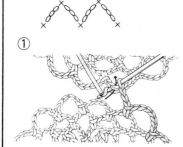

①

②

③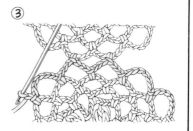

BASIC CROCHET STITCHES

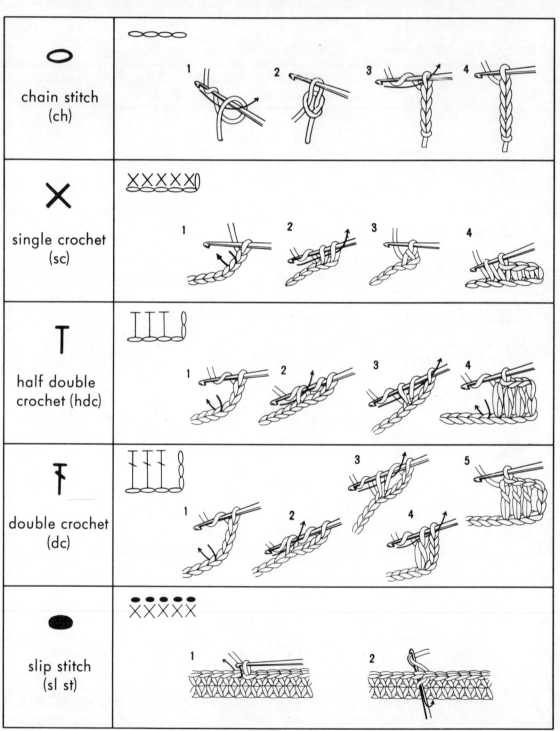

chain stitch (ch)	
single crochet (sc)	
half double crochet (hdc)	
double crochet (dc)	
slip stitch (sl st)	